This is a must-read book because..

- ✓ You want to know how to deal with anxiety

- ✓ You want to control your panic attacks

- ✓ You want to know how to deal with overwhelming thoughts and feelings

- ✓ You want to release your guilty feelings

- ✓ You want practical strategies to help with Stress, Overwhelm and Guilt (SOG)

- ✓ You want to make better choices

- ✓ You want to help yourself

- ✓ You want to take control of your life

- ✓ You want to be more confident

- ✓ You want to feel happy

Fear Less Live More

Sometimes happiness is being a fish out of water...

Andrea A Smith

BOOK BRILLIANCE
P U B L I S H I N G

First published in Great Britain in 2020
by Book Brilliance Publishing
265A Fir Tree Road, Epsom, Surrey, KT17 3LF
+44 (0)20 8641 5090
www.bookbrilliancepublishing.com
admin@bookbrilliancepublishing.com

A CIP catalogue record for this book is available at the British Library.

ISBN 978-1-913770-01-3
Typeset in Calibri
Printed in Great Britain by 4edge Ltd

This book is not intended as a substitute for the medical advice of
physicians. The reader should regularly consult a physician in matters
relating to his/her health and particularly with respect to
any symptoms that may require diagnosis or medical attention.

Words of Love

I first met Andrea when we studied together for a Bachelor of Science degree in Clinical Hypnosis at St Mary's University in Twickenham, London.

Andrea's desire to help people overcome fear and anxiety to enable them to achieve their life goals, was apparent in her every action.

Andrea had conquered her own fears to enable her to give her own children the life that she wanted for them and was doing this as a single parent, studying and working full time as a nurse in a busy hospital.

In writing this book, Andrea's passion for helping people shows, as she continues on her quest to free people from fear, anxiety and panic. I wish her all the very best in all that she is doing. All power and love to you and all those whose lives you are helping, Andrea.

Freddy Jacquin
Book Author, Trainer and Speaker
https://freddyjacquin.com/

Andrea really does live more by fearing less and has certainly spurred me on when I might have allowed opportunities to pass me by. She successfully motivates and inspires her clients to persistently take the actions needed to enjoy personal, transformative life experiences. A warm, vibrant personality and a strong work ethic means

Andrea is a force for change. When I need a helping hand, I reach out to Andrea; she cares, offering safe passage through troubling parts of life. Andrea's book *Fear Less, Live More* can help you create your best life as easily as A, B, C, … D and E!

Caroline Anderson
Author, Coach and Speaker
withcaroline.com

This superb little book is a mine of information and approaches to be adopted in considering the universal problem of stress and how to deal with it.

With a plethora of helpful quotes and individual case histories to consider, together with the author's own shattering life experiences, you will complete your read feeling lighter and more positive, even before starting to put into practice her own unique and original methods of dealing with the anxiety, panic attacks and doubts about self-esteem that afflict us all at some time or another in our lives.

Read it. And see for yourself.

Highly recommended.

R. Andrew Segal
Author of 'The Lyme Regis Murders' and Business Owner
andrewsegalauthor.com/

Working with Andrea has been a joy. It is a dream to collaborate and co-create something deep and meaningful based on authenticity, passion and expertise. *Fear Less, Live More* provides the reader with stories and theory, backed up by lots of practical tips. Andrea demonstrated great courage by opening her heart and soul through her vulnerability and honesty to share her story. This is not a stuffy read but one that offers the reader practical solutions within each chapter. The generosity of Andrea is also illustrated in her accompanying workbook. Andrea's mission is to make a difference in people's lives and through her own challenges, she has learned there is a way to Fear Less and Live More.

Brenda Dempsey
Publisher – Book Brilliance Publishing

If anxiety, stress and overwhelm has taken hold in your life, this book is a must. You will feel understood, supported but most of all, you will leave with strategies and solutions that are effective and easy to put into place.

I love the stories, the simplicity of the layout and the relatability to the author. Reading this book will give you choices that maybe you didn't realise you had.

So pick up a handful of courage, follow the guidance and step into what is possible instead of what isn't... And breathe into the freedom of life.

Fiona Clark
The Zenergizer
www.fionaclark.co.uk

How do we know what love is
When we don't even understand ourselves?
Have opinions about what is love and what love is not,
When all our actions are absent of love?

Where do we go when we feel separated, fragmented and
alone in this world,
How do we find peace, comfort and love
What is the truth that we need to know,
So we can find our way back home to where we belong?
So take a moment, stop and consider,
The possibility that we are love and all that means
That every action is a result of loving oneself
Even if we don't understand the means

And trust that when we move in towards ourselves,
And listen quietly to the gentle whisper of our soul
We get to learn who we really are
LOVE ITSELF

Sherine Lovegrove
Author, Transformational Coach and Psychotherapist
www.sherinelovegrove.com

Contents

Foreword

S tress, overwhelm and guilt are emotions we, as human beings, find ourselves experiencing more and more. For some, this can be crippling and not enable them to get on with their lives. As a coach myself, I regularly see clients who experience these issues and work with them to find a new way forward.

Andrea A Smith is a stress resilience coach who has used her own adversity and dark days to support and help others manage stress and develop their resilience.

Her experience of relationship breakdown, being a single mother and having to rebuild her life, have been the catalyst to her work helping others who find themselves governed by fear, anxiety, stress, overwhelm and guilt.

Stress and anxiety are huge issues in our society causing problems ranging from time off work to ill health; being able to understand the causes and our behaviours enables us to move forward and lead rich lives.

Andrea has a wealth of experience which is channelled into *Fear Less, Live More*, enabling you to delve into your emotions and find a way out of darkness into light. Her own experience illuminates the text, along with case studies and tools showing how you too can make a change and fear less.

Each chapter covers an emotion in depth and shows ways to deepen your understanding of the issue and change your relationship with stress, anxiety and overwhelm. As you read each chapter, you can reflect and engage with the exercises to begin your personal journey of transformation.

Dr Yvette Ankrah MBE
Transformational Coach
www.yvetteankrah.com
yvette@yvetteankrah.com

Introduction

Choosing to write *Fear Less, Live More* was an easy decision. The challenge was how I was going to share everything with you that I had inside my mind, body and soul. I knew I had to reveal my blood, sweat and tears on this wonderful journey called life, as well as all the joy I have found along the way that has brought me to this point.

I was born and raised in India from a poor background. Despite this, I was determined from a young age that I was going to make something of myself and my life. In one defining moment, I decided to kick fear into touch. Sure, I was frightened, but my 'WHY' was bigger than me! I have learned that having a significant WHY is a vital element to achieving success, and living a free and happy life.

After many battles with my parents, I became a nurse. It felt good at first, but I soon lost my way. Part of that devastating journey was when I found myself on the other side of the world in New Zealand with two small children. Although there was trepidation, I felt excited until my husband abandoned us and then I felt lost.

The battle had begun. Somehow I found my way back to the UK to start all over again as a single mother of two children. There were tears, fear and exhaustion. Being human, I wanted to throw in the towel, yet something stopped me. Determined to understand the human mind, I decided to embark on a Masters in Psychology degree. It seemed the more I was hurting and exhausted, the more determined I was to change my life for the better.

As a nurse, I cared for many women who were suffering and struggling like me, except they were on pills, drugs and all sorts of things that deadened them even more inside. They deserved better but they did not know what to do or how to do it. I was not content with completing my Masters in Psychology so I went on and learned more tools to help me work with women to change their lives for the better from the inside out.

I am the evidence of what is possible. I am proof of such transformation and that has driven me to write *Fear Less, Live More*. The biggest block to people moving forward is Fear. In my book, I discuss Stress, Overwhelm and Guilt (SOG) in detail, as well as the impact of anxiety and panic attacks. But that is not enough, so I have also made this book interactive by using the power of Narrative Questioning and provoking thoughts that will enable you to change.

You will find the book easy to read and follow due to its familiar structure, subheadings and its activities. I have chosen to weave challenging experiences from my life throughout the book, enhanced by the use of stories, metaphors and case studies to illustrate what is possible for you too.

As you read this book, I encourage you to grab a notebook, and if you have purchased this book from my website you will be fortunate enough to have received the free PDF download that accompanies it. You will discover throughout the book that we use jotting down and journaling as a way to release negativity and create space for reframing your mindset and shifting perception. The results are significant and this practical strategy is a life-changer. I know it was, and still is, for me.

Are you ready for the journey? Let's begin...

Andrea A Smith

CHAPTER ONE
Losing Control

'Fears are nothing more than a state of mind.'

Napoleon Hill
Author of 'Think and Grow Rich'

Fear is defined as 'an unpleasant emotion caused by the threat of danger, pain, or harm.'
(O.E.D)

Fear is a natural survival mechanism. Humans have been surviving since time began, when we would run away, stay and fight, or simply freeze with fright. Fear can occur when you see something as a threat, such as when your boss unexpectedly calls you into their office for a meeting. Your body responds biochemically and emotionally to try and protect itself.

Most of us feel fear at some point or other in our lives, as a result of our experiences, some past trauma or when we lose control in different situations. We fear many things, from lack of money, redundancy and illness, to the unknown, especially when it is exacerbated by stress. In this heightened negative state, we release chemicals, mainly cortisol, in our brain, leading to an increased heart rate, rapid breathing and negative mind chatter. Living in a sustained state of fear creates dis-ease within our bodies.

Within the brain, the prefrontal cortex, amygdala and hippocampus all process fear. The prefrontal cortex will filter the incoming fear, and the hippocampus will receive and recall the memories of the pain stored in your subconscious mind. Next, the amygdala will translate emotions to check for the threat, and finally, the hippocampus will activate the response 'flight, fight or freeze'.

In the survival response, you may feel as if you are losing control, tricking your thoughts and feelings into believing they are real. Even though you may not be in any physical danger, you may still feel threatened. You are building a fictitious picture for yourself, and this false perception creates anxiety as you try to predict outcomes.

Following on from your boss inviting you into their office for an unexpected meeting, en route your mind will be scrambling to find a reason for this situation. As a typical human reaction, your first thoughts turn to 'What have I done wrong? Am I going to be reprimanded even though I know I've done nothing wrong?' But for all you know, your boss may just want to tell you about a new project!

There is a gap between the starting point – your boss asking you to go to their office – and the final point – telling you about the new project. The gap is the uncertainty of what is going to happen. It is a part of living in a challenging universe with no guarantee, so you ruminate and worry about things and feel as if you have lost control.

Welcome to the world of living with anxiety. Anxiety is fearfulness of the future.

Prefrontal Cortex
The Centre that regulates your thoughts, emotions and actions. Very vulnerable to an increase in brain chemicals caused by stress.

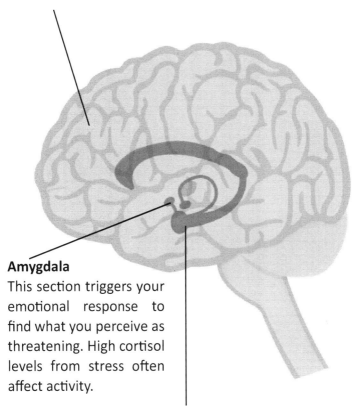

Amygdala
This section triggers your emotional response to find what you perceive as threatening. High cortisol levels from stress often affect activity.

Hippocampus
The hippocampus has a major role in learning and memory, and connects the emotion of fear to the threatening event. Again, high levels of cortisol from stress affect growth and performance.

> **'It is our light, not our darkness,
> that most frightens us. Our fear is
> a mixture of our worrying thoughts
> and is not real.'**
> *Andrea Smith*

For me to write this book, I must firstly present my fears to you. I too have experienced fear on many occasions throughout my life. Most prominent was the experience of travelling to the other side of the planet, only to be separated within a few short months.

In 2006, I immigrated to New Zealand because my husband wanted our children to grow up in a more settled and relaxed atmosphere with an outdoor lifestyle. I travelled to New Zealand with my children ahead of my husband. After we had lived there for six months, my marriage abruptly ended. This situation intensified as my husband had still not immigrated to New Zealand. My world blew apart. My heart broke into a million pieces. I had never felt pain and fear like that before. I was fearful about my financial security, my kids' future, my life and my home (as I had no home now in the UK). My life partner had left me alone to bring up our kids. I had lost everything, including the next three days. The fear was all-consuming. All I could do was scream. The terror came in waves, and sometimes I felt okay, and at other times the fear was so intense that I reeled with the pain. Sometimes I crumbled on the floor with the agony; and even worse was that I had to keep the trauma a secret as my kids needed me. The fear ravaged me; stopped me from laughing, being happy, living, relaxing and moving forward.

♦ YOUR TURN

Identify your biggest fear. It could be now or an episode in your past when you experienced extreme fear. Grab your journal or notepad, and write down how you felt, and then let it go as you exhale it from your body through writing.

♦ DANCING WITH WOLVES

There is an old leader of a faraway tribe who is teaching the children of the village about life.

He tells them, 'A struggle is going on inside me. A terrible struggle and it is a struggle between two wolves.

'One wolf represents fear, greed, hatred, anger, envy, false pride, self-pity, resentment, guilt, inferiority, arrogance, deceitfulness, superiority and selfishness.

'The other wolf stands for peace, love, kindness, joy, truth, compassion, humility, transparency, authenticity, friendship, respect, integrity, benevolence, generosity, faith, sharing, serenity and empathy.

'The same struggle is happening inside of you and in every other person as well.'

For a while, the children consider what they are hearing. Suddenly one small child asks the leader, 'Which wolf will win?'

The old leader looks at the child for some time then answers, 'Whichever one you feed.'

GENERAL SOURCE: Native American tradition

◆ METAPHOR LESSONS

Decisions begin within you, when you reflect on what you think is right and proper in your world view. Decisions are based on your values and beliefs, and can often be rooted in your culture. As leaders of your own lives, you begin with <u>Your</u> integrity. Each of you has battles within, and the wolves in the story represent good and bad decisions which then cause a negative or positive attitude in your lives. We all have choices, and depending on your experiences and responses, you make your decisions – good or bad. When you choose to ignore fear and focus on love instead, you create a win-win situation for you, your friends and family, and the world. The choices you make in your mind will determine the reality you experience. Know that struggle is a natural part of being human and your choice can make all the difference to the quality of your life.

◆ A PHILOSOPHY UNFOLDING

Fear often leads to stress and overwhelm, and can come in waves at any time of the day or night. The unknown factor of when the pain will come, is like the ebbing and flowing of the sea. It fills your mind with panic, anxiety and doubt.

 Panic is a strong feeling of fear which can immobilise you, preventing thought and action.

 Anxiety is a feeling of fear, unease and intense worry, which leads to loss of control.

 Doubt is a feeling of uncertainty about things and fear when you are stressed.

You fear *losing control* when struck by the emotional waves of suppression. So it is time to consider owning your feelings and gaining control of your fears the best way you can. WHY? Admitting your feeling is the first step of taking back control and getting your thoughts and life back to normal. You can write your fears and ideas down in a diary, which can be used as a form of healing, accepting and letting go of those thoughts. The thoughts themselves do not harm you, but it is the emotion attached to those thoughts, and their repetition for days, weeks, months and even years that impact your behaviour.

'What if I panic in front of my guests?' 'What if I fumble with my words and look like a fool?' 'What will my family think of me if my fiancé leaves me?' are all fears you may have when you feel you have lost control. You will experience knots in your stomach, have infinite worries and seemingly have no control over future events, which can leave you feeling extremely frightened.

Many of us like to be in control of our thoughts, so as to be sure about our future. Understanding and challenging the root cause of these fearful thoughts is the first step, and then learning how to feel calm when you are feeling fear and using positive self-talk can help. Implementing these strategies can make you believe you are achieving what you desire and will boost your self-esteem, making you in control of any fear and stress that follows on.

Do you know that you have approximately 60,000 thoughts every day and that 95% of those thoughts are the same? This notion reminds me of what the great Albert Einstein said,

'Insanity is doing the same thing over and over again and expecting different results.'

Once you become aware of how to understand and deal with the fear and anxiety, then you have moved into a different paradigm; you cannot unlearn new things. This breakthrough encourages growth within you. Understanding fear is the beginning of ridding yourself of it for good. (Well, as good as you can handle!) No matter what, the subconscious mind will always allow fear to rear its head from time to time, especially when you have to learn a new lesson, are under pressure or tired. That is fine as, over time, you will develop strategies that allow you to deal with fear head-on. This significant change in your thought patterns and behaviour will enable you to embrace fear and exert your power over it. This is what you are working towards. There is no place for concern when you have a WHY bigger than you. More about that later.

♦ DO DIFFERENT TO CREATE CHANGE

The Alphabet Method

I want to share with you one of my methodologies. After a number of years working with a wide range of clients, as well as conducting research and gaining knowledge, I created the **Alphabet Method**. I was able to see a pattern emerging in both my clients and my own work that allowed both myself and my clients to take control and work through a process that would create the change we all seek in our life.

The Alphabet Method enables you to find the cause of your fear step by step, thus giving you the courage to do something different; you then practise your new-found skill so that it becomes part of your new behaviour and achieves the results you desire.

A	B	C	D	E
(Be alert)	(Take a breath)	(Check what you are reacting to)	(Dispute/ challenge your thoughts)	(Effective practice of what works)
Be alert to your triggers and recognise them. *Jot them down.*	Mindful Breathing: Breathe deeply, slowly and calmly. *Breathe deeply, slowly and calmly. Try 7-11 breathing (breathe in slowly for the count of 7 and out for the count of 11).*	What is causing you to be stressed, anxious or worried? What are the circulating thoughts saying or what do they mean? How are the thoughts affecting you, i.e. the physical sensation you notice in your body? Where is the focus of your attention? *Take time to leave your worry aside.*	Are these thoughts fact or opinion? Can you see this situation as a curious scientist or an observer? What advice would you give a friend if she had the same problem? Think of the energy that you are giving to a thought – what is making you react in this manner? What are the consequences of the thought? *Instead of avoiding the challenge, you can jot down an alternative response.*	Practice what works: What can I do right now? I don't need to check or seek reassurance. *1. Negative Thoughts record sheet.* *2. Postpone your worry or set a worry-free time.* *3. Mindful breathing.* *4. Overcome avoidance.* *5. Mindful activity.*

Be Alert > Breathe > Check > Dispute > Effect

♦ **YOUR TURN**

Use the previous explanation to help you connect within and find your answers. It's time to create change.

A – Be Alert	
B – Breathe	
C – Check	
D – Dispute	
E – Effect	

Martha's Story – Martha's husband left her in the worse possible way... she told him that she felt he was into some weird sexual stuff and as she could no longer satisfy him, he left her for another woman after 23 years of marriage. Martha was in debt, and left with two kids and a part-time job. The situation she found herself in had left a gaping hole and she started to spin out of control with fear and anxiety about money, her image, her confidence, her relationship and her home. Feeling crushed by so many issues, she could not think straight. She was not sleeping, she ate badly and sporadically, and there was no structure to her day.

What we did – Talking Therapy including Systemic Constellation Coaching. We explored and identified her past childhood learned patterns of behaviour from her parents. Using the Alphabet Method, Martha was able to regain control of her fear of the unknown. Narrative Questioning allowed Martha to distance and detach herself from her story. By using self-reflection and journaling, along with the 1-10 Scale, she was able to move from fear to calm, thus creating new patterns of behaviour and change.

Result – She is now conscious of what she is feeling fearful about and has started to take small steps to be positive, including having the courage to make new friends in the area where she moved to. She contacted old friends and now has a circle of support and help.

♦ THE POWER OF NARRATIVE QUESTIONING

Narrative Questioning

Teaching and learning cannot happen without questions. Questions are incredibly powerful tools that open up the world. One vital area where Narrative Questioning plays a significant role is in 'The Story of Your Life'. We all like to tell people stories about our life. Your mood, perspective and mindset will determine whether you are the Hero or the Victim.

The goal is to distance and detach yourself from the story. Using Narrative Questioning is a vital tool in understanding more about yourself, your problems and the stories you tell yourself.

There is a set of Narrative Question starter words that can help you determine effective questioning techniques. These words preclude open and closed questions. Writers often use Narrative Questions as the term 'Narrative' suggests a story. That is what we tell ourselves and others every day. Using these Narrative Questions can change and shape the story we want to tell ourselves and others. Narrative Questioning is very useful for relieving stress, overwhelm and guilt that cause anxiety and fear.

What? When? Who? Why? Where? How?

If?...then

Here are a few examples:

❖ How long have you been noticing this [problem]?

❖ What effect does it have on your life?

❖ Why is this? Why are you taking this position on what [the problem] is doing?

Are these effects acceptable to you or not?

If you were to stay connected to what you have just said about what you prefer, what next steps could you take?

♦ **THE IMPACT OF THREATS**

Your brain routinely gets tricked into making mistakes, such as overestimating threats from events and situations that make your frightened. Extreme stress, fear and worry can cause your mind to be wary and vigilant, so understanding how the brain works and responds is the first step to gain control. You can feel vulnerable when you feel threatened, and this can affect you on many levels. For example, you may overestimate the threat of how your parents will react when you tell them what career option you want to take in the future. You may hesitate to start a new business venture, or take that road trip you've planned. Here are a number of the ways some of us overestimate threats and what will actually happen:

♦ **THE FOUR 'I's OF OVERESTIMATING THE THREAT:**

1. **Implausible (you overthink the threat, but it's unlikely to happen)**

2. **Improbable (it's doubtful that what you think will happen)**

3. Inconceivable (you have imagined that the worst is true, but it's not)

4. Incredible (it's impossible that your fears will materialise)

When your brain responds to the threat, you can build a neural pathway in your mind by being mindfully aware of what you are reacting to, or what is the cause of the threat. This conscious action will bring a sense of calm, develop your inner strength and self-esteem, and your behaviour will start to banish the threat and the fear that comes with it. Below are some of your reactions to the danger and fear:

A. Catastrophising – you predict or jump to conclusions with negative outcomes

B. Overgeneralising – worsening of your thoughts and feelings that you cannot do anything right

C. Overreacting – responding to something with unnecessary emotion

D. Fortune telling – you predict a negative future

E. Mind reading – you believe that you know what the other person is thinking and it is not positive

You need to consider whether your fears are valid or whether you have exaggerated them in your mind. Ask yourself what is the benefit of beating that fearful drum.

The questions to ask yourself:

How INTENSE is Fear in your current problem? (where 0 is negligible and 10 is intense)

How intense is the wish to change your fear and become calm? (where 0 is negligible and 10 is intense)

What is the likelihood you will take action? (where 0 is negligible and 10 is intense)

♦ **SUMMARY**

When FEAR consumes you, it is easy to lose control. The first thing is to understand it and then awaken your awareness of its impact on you. Once you face fear head-on, you can begin to change your thinking, behaviour and life. Tools laid out in this chapter, such as Self-Reflection,

Journaling, Narrative Questioning, and 1-10 Scale, can support you as you transition from FEAR to CALM. Well done! You have taken the first step!

Andrea's Learning Alerts to zap your Fear!

❖ Fear is not real.

❖ Awareness creates change.

❖ You can change the way you think.

❖ You can change your response and behaviour.

❖ Your choices make all the difference to the quality of your life.

❖ Breathing helps you to connect within and calm down.

❖ Ask Narrative Questions on the 1-10 Scale.

CHAPTER TWO
Gaining Control

'Anxiety and Panic Attacks are not signs of weakness. They are signs of trying to remain strong for too long.'

**'Our anxiety does not come from thinking about
the future, but from wanting to control it.'**
Kahlil Gibran
Best-selling author of 'The Prophet'

♦ **ANXIETY**

S tress is a life factor that you have come to take for granted. Stress is often associated with situations you perceive as difficult to handle.

Researchers define stress as a physical, mental, or emotional response that causes bodily or mental tension. Simply put, it is an outside force or event that affects your body or mind.

Most of the factors that cause stress are external; they come from the outside world. External factors include things such as job pressures, family life, relationships, physical illnesses and significant events that happen to you or your loved ones. The list of stress factors is endless.

Have you ever worried about the future and how you are going to cope when your life significantly changes, such as getting divorced, facing redundancy or fear of getting ill? One of the main factors that cause your anxiety is that you do not have control of the whole situation. Hence, uncertainty is the main culprit of your anxiety. Most people experience this at some time in their life.

When you fear about the future, you experience anxiety, and we each differently feel the way our bodies respond to being in perceived danger. It's your body's alarm mechanism. Consider the threat of being caught in a fire or imagining you are going to crash on a flight, and your body prepares for danger, real or perceived. In that instant, you activate the fight-flight-freeze response. The body's alarm system is simple. Challenged with a sense of danger, even the ordinary everyday type of a perceived fearful situation like a crowded train, the fight-flight-freeze response is triggered. Now the body wants to fight the circumstances, run away or freeze like a rabbit in headlights.

The word anxiety describes thoughts and feelings of worry, fear and unease felt within your body. According to the UK charity Mind, anxiety is what we feel when we are worried, tense or afraid. When you live with intense anxiety, you develop a heightened sensitivity to your environment. You are in continuous scanning mode, looking for danger signals or imagining the worst thing is going to happen, increasing your hyper-alertness to everything.

Many people experience anxiety at some point in their lives. Instead of taking comfort from this knowledge, you think you are the only person experiencing your anxious situation. The fear of judgement overrides your sensibility and intensifies the anxiety. During this time, you may have sleepless nights, physical symptoms and find it hard to eat. These feelings will stop after the situation passes. However, if your feelings of anxiety are intense, they may last for a prolonged time, creating a strong overwhelm. At the extreme, it affects your ability to live your life in a relaxed manner.

♦ PANIC ATTACKS

Mind explains that panic attacks can happen during the day or night. Ignored anxiety may escalate. In some cases, a panic attack ensues, which is the body's response to intense fear. In these situations, your body triggers a physical reaction which is severe, even when there may be no apparent cause of danger.

Research shows that if you do not address the cause of panic attacks, you are more likely to experience it again, when you find yourself in the same or similar circumstances. You may even find yourself in a cycle of panic attacks. If not interrupted, the neural pathways laid down will create a new negative learned behaviour.

Stress factors are the anxiety and panic attacks you feel, leading to the fight-flight-freeze-fawn response. It is the body's automatic, built-in system designed to protect you from threat or danger.

♦ MY STORY

I would like to walk you further through my journey so you can understand my anxiety and panic. My experience was activated when faced with one of the toughest times in my life – returning from New Zealand after my marriage breakdown.

When I returned from NZ to the UK, I stayed with a friend first, but she felt she could not support me as her marital relationship was also weak. I was heartbroken and hurt as I needed to process my situation. I began struggling with anxiety and then panic as I had to set up home again. I worried if I could cope. I was a single mum. I had friends, but none that came and took the kids off me, giving me the space to heal and recover. I rented a flat for the kids and me. About six months after moving back to the UK and finding my feet… I found me. I was a mother and a wife and cook, cleaner, gardener, I worked (juggling work-family life), but for the last few years, I had lost a part of me. Now I was on my own, and I found the lost me. My likes and dislikes, how I wanted to dress up, be me, and make my choice on what kind of television programs I wanted to watch. I felt free for the first time in my life. I felt like a woman again and went back to university, to hunger for learning. I also had personal therapy and took time to process.

♦ YOUR TURN

Go to your notebook/workbook. Identify a problem you overcame. Using Narrative Questions – What did you do? How did you feel? Why did things change for you? Journal it out without judgement. Come back after you have completed this activity.

Anxiety is like walking down a dark and scary alley without knowing what is waiting for you.

When anxiety floods your mind, you are more concerned with endings or outcomes – fearing the unknown and the future is an everyday occurrence. Many people worry about household bills as they are a significant threat to your sense of mental and physical serenity, and these are vital. It is beneficial to understand that you cannot control the future. Accepting this as truth arouses your curiosity to think wisely about how you can work towards achieving smaller steps to your goal rather than the end itself. For example, when you want to climb a staircase, you must consider each step (i.e. the actual stairs) before reaching the top – each step is governed by the pace suitable for the walker, not society.

◆ UNFOLDING PHILOSOPHY: ANXIETY AND PANIC ATTACKS

◆ PART ONE: ANXIETY – a feeling of worry, nervousness, or unease about something with an uncertain outcome.

Anxiety is experienced through your thoughts, feelings and physical sensations when you think about a situation that is not your reality. It happens when you think about what could happen in the future. Some people view anxiety as part of everyday life. However, according to *Psychology Today*, it is when persistent, pervasive anxiety disrupts one's daily life, whether at home, work or with friends, that indicates an 'anxiety disorder'. In light of my experience, training and learning, anxiety is a natural human response when we perceive that we are under threat. Indeed, anxiety is that uneasy feeling when you consider the total loss of control of your thoughts, feelings and senses.

Triggers for anxiety come in the form of unhelpful thoughts and feelings. They may include:

❖ Something that is happening right now.

❖ Something that occurred in the past.

❖ Something you are anticipating will happen in the future.

❖ Something like an object, place, person, which causes you to get anxious.

❖ Something like an image or a memory, which causes you anxiety.

❖ Something like a physical sensation, such as increased heart rate, headaches or feeling tired continually, causing you to be anxious about your health.

These thoughts and beliefs can be terrifying. *Raising your awareness and understanding is the first step to creating change.*

The activating event or the trigger evokes a rush of emotional feeling and unhelpful thoughts:

Your behaviours or the consequences of the thoughts and beliefs could be ill health, unable to move up the career ladder or find a partner as well as many more.

The negative thoughts go round and round, you lose perspective, and these thoughts can be toxic – causing you to feel destructive emotions. Unreliable destructive emotions can prevent you from asking your present boss for a rise, fearing you will get rejected or are not good enough. It can also prevent you from achieving a career change that you love and would make you feel better, but you are too scared even to try.

Another negative response to panic attacks is procrastination due to the negative thoughts about achieving a goal, such as a college degree. You are shrouded in doubts and worries. Consequently, these thoughts produce unpleasant feelings and emotions within you, making you anxious, stressed or depressed. In this disempowering state, your daily routines are disturbed, leaving you feeling discouraged. These thoughts trick you into believing you are a failure, and consequently, you feel down and may even give up.

One of the ways you can feel relief from anxiety is to understand how it works. Keeping your emotions separate from your thoughts and realising what you feel inside is not necessarily a correct assessment of what you perceive the situation to be in reality. In other words, your mind can fool you into believing that your worst nightmare is about to happen. The issue is that your anxiety is in control, and when you feel out of sync or not in control, this triggers your anxiety.

Introducing the Anxiety Loop

The Anxiety Loop is what happens when you experience heightened anxiety. You enter a cycle – the Anxiety Loop – and unless the pattern breaks, you will remain in this psychological state. It is essential to know that your anxiety affects you physically, and over time, can cause dis-ease and a state of negative mental well-being.

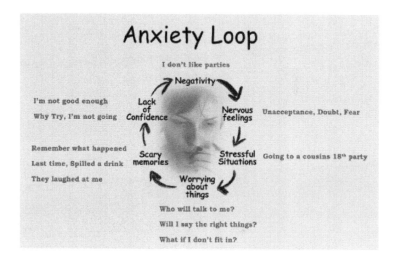

For example, you will avoid going to your cousin's 18th birthday party because you don't feel comfortable with her friends. This *negativity* affects your decision-making. The birthday party soon becomes your only thought and fuels *nervous feelings* laden with notions of unacceptance, doubt and fear. Consequently, you label parties as a *stressful situation*. Next, your imagination starts to create scenarios that only played out in your mind as *worrying things*, such as questions, 'Who will talk to me?' 'What if

I don't fit in?' 'What if I spill something?' Your mind then relapses back to the past of a *scary memory* when you spilt a drink down yourself. You begin to build a scenario that leads to a *lack of confidence* confirming your false belief that parties are adverse. So you convince yourself, 'I don't like parties.'

When you enter a cycle of negativity, your thoughts become irrational, illogical and unrealistic. Consequently, thoughts lead to self-defeating and harmful thinking patterns. You might worry about the shoes you hastily put on for evening drinks with friends, and you discover they do not match your dress. Irrational thoughts may lead you to think that people judge you.

♦ **PART TWO: PANIC ATTACKS – a physical and emotional response to the intense fear of something.**

According to the National Health Service (NHS), a panic attack is when your body experiences a rush of intense mental and physical symptoms. It can come on very quickly and for no apparent reason. A panic attack can be very frightening and distressing.

During a panic attack, you can hear your heart pounding; you feel as if you cannot breathe properly and as if you are going crazy. Panic attacks can cause some symptoms like shaking, a sense of impending doom and abdominal pain. A single panic attack can last for a few minutes, or be prolonged. It can take an emotional toll where the memory can leave its imprint and can cause severe disruption to your daily life. If not dealt with, you will then avoid certain situations believing that you can also avoid another panic attack.

Some people have one panic attack then never experience another. On the other hand, you might find that you have them regularly, or several in a short space of time. Perhaps you notice that particular places, situations or activities seem to trigger panic attacks. For example, they might happen before a stressful appointment.

The physical symptoms of panic attacks cause the body's fight-flight-freeze-fawn response to the feelings of anxiety and fear.

Most panic attacks last between 5–20 minutes. They can come on very quickly. Your symptoms will usually peak (be at their worst) within 10 minutes. You might also experience symptoms of a panic attack over a more extended period. One explanation is you may experience a second panic attack, or you're suffering other anxiety symptoms.

♦   PART THREE: ANXIETY AND PANIC ATTACKS

As anxiety and panic attacks are a stress response in the body, it all starts in your mind. During a fight-flight-freeze reaction, many physiological changes occur. The train of reaction begins in your amygdala, the part of your brain responsible for perceived fear. The amygdala responds by sending signals to the hypothalamus, which stimulates the autonomic nervous system (ANS).

These changes allow you to act so you can protect yourself. It's a survival instinct that our ancestors developed many years ago.

Panic Attack Anxiety	Anxiety
• **Heart rate.** Your heart beats faster to bring oxygen to your major muscles. • **Lungs.** Your breathing speeds up to deliver more oxygen to your blood. • **Eyes.** Your peripheral vision increases so you can notice your surroundings. • **Ears.** Your ears 'perk up' and your hearing becomes sharper. • **Blood.** Blood thickens, which increases clotting factors preparing your body for injury. • **Skin.** Your skin might produce more sweat or get cold. You may look pale or have goosebumps. • **Hands and feet.** As blood flow increases to your major muscles, your hands and feet might get cold. • **Pain perception.** Fight-or-flight temporarily reduces your perception of pain.	• **A sense of doom,** affecting your ability to concentrate. • **Depression** including social isolation, loss of interest and feelings of guilt. • **Headaches** from constant fear and worry, increasing your **irritability**. • **Pounding heart** with increased pace and intensity. • **Breathing problems.** Rapid and shallow breathing. • **Upset stomach** causing pain, nausea or diarrhoea. • **Loss of libido.** Decreased sex drive. • **Extreme fatigue** leaving you feeling wiped out. • **Increase blood pressure.** You may feel your blood pressure rise when anxious. • **Aches and pains.** Anxiety is not merely mental; it can cause physical symptoms too.

The hormones cortisol and epinephrine (also known as adrenaline, the primary fight or flight hormone) are released when the body experiences stress. The intoxicating impact of these **stress hormones** on the body results in disabling physical symptoms and dis-ease. It is time to change your thinking.

Fight, Flight, Freeze, and Fawn – What is it?

Walter Bradford Cannon, Chair of Physiology at Harvard in the 1920s, coined the term Fight or Flight response, explaining what he called the 'acute stress response'. Many physiologists and psychologists have continued to build on and refine Cannon's work and have come to a deeper understanding of how people react to threats. They have introduced two new responses, Freeze and Fawn. You may not be familiar with the terms.

1. **Fight** – confront threats aggressively.

2. **Flight** – run from the danger.

3. **Freeze** – you are rooted to the spot, unable to move or act against the threat.

4. **Fawn** – a response of complying with the attacker to save yourself.

The fight-flight-freeze-fawn response is a choice and has much to do with your beliefs. If you believe you can conquer the danger, your body will jump into fight mode. But if you think there's no hope of defeating the attacker, you'll naturally respond by running away. There has been much research over the years about Fight or Flight.

Consider when someone gets trapped under a weight. Those who Fight will find the extraordinary strength to raise the weight so that the injured person can be pulled to safety.

When you hear the words, 'Look out!' you may be surprised to find how fast you take Flight. You feel grateful as you narrowly miss a flying football sailing above your head, as your son is playing football in the back garden!

More recently, there have been studies into the Freeze response. Scientists from the University of Bristol has discovered the pathways that regulate freezing responses. In their results, they argue that this response could be instrumental in helping people overcome certain disorders. When researchers investigated where these pathways led, they found themselves in a separate region, known as the pyramid. Specifically, when innate and learnt threatening situations were at play (those being either survival modes or aversions to certain noises), the pyramid lit up.

When you freeze, like a rabbit in headlights, when you are climbing a high set of steps, you perceive it as a threat or feel that you are in danger when you reach a certain height. Your thoughts turn to impending doom. Next, your breathing becomes fast and shallow. You think you are having a heart attack. Even though you know this thought is irrational, you cannot accept the reality of the situation. You feel that the danger is real, and your response is simply to freeze.

The Fawn response can happen when you can't fight or run. Instead, you choose to go along, trying to win over a person who is abusing or manipulating you. This is also known as the Stockholm Syndrome.

It is one thing to understand the responses you might have when you feel threatened. What helps the most is being able to recognise each type of answer. Only then can you find a way.

How to recognise Fight, Flight, Freeze or Fawn Response

Fight

When faced with danger, the 'Fight' response kicks in. You experience an incredible belief that you can conquer the threat. Your brain sends messages to your muscles to quickly prepare and get ready for the physical demands of fighting. Some of the signs you are in fight mode include:

❖ You have an urge to punch someone or something

❖ Your jaw tenses, or you grind your teeth

❖ You scowl at others or your voice rises with anger

❖ You feel like stomping around like a child

❖ You feel livid

❖ You have no control as tears run down your face

❖ Your thoughts turn to harming someone or yourself

❖ Your stomach churns, leaving you feeling nauseated

You'll be in no doubt that you are in fight mode as you want to attack the threat. The fight response is tremendously favourable under certain circumstances.

Flight

Your innate response to danger may be to run away. In these circumstances, your brain prepares your body for Flight. Sometimes, running away is your best decision. If you're not a firefighter, you undoubtedly run out of a burning building. Here are some of the emotional and physical flight responses:

❖ Your legs and feet are restless

❖ You feel numbness in your extremities

❖ Your pupils dilate and dart around

❖ You're fidgety

- ❖ You're tense

- ❖ You feel trapped

- ❖ Your mouth is dry

- ❖ You sweat profusely

- ❖ Your skin tone changes

Freeze

When neither running away nor staying to fight are the best options, you may find yourself freezing. The following freeze responses can keep you stuck:

- ❖ You feel cold

- ❖ Your body feels numb

- ❖ You feel stiff or heavy

- ❖ You have a sense of dread

- ❖ Your heart is pounding

- ❖ Your heart rate may decrease

- ❖ You think yourself tolerating the stress

Fawn

Fawning is usually associated with people who tend to come from abusive relationships or situations.

If you've experienced abuse, compliance with your abuser may be your only hope of survival. You can recognise this, but despite how badly you are being treated, your primary concern is keeping them happy rather than protecting yourself.

ANXIETY RESPONSE TO PANIC

The anxiety response to panic plays a crucial role when faced with danger. Sometimes anxiety or panic can trigger the fight-flight-freeze-fawn response even if there is no real threat or danger, but it is perceived. You enter the Anxiety Loop (see page 47).

Your fight-flight-freeze-fawn response may occur in an everyday situation, such as when you are out for a walk with a friend. As you come around the curve in the road, you are faced with a bulldog. The response is triggered because you are scared of dogs, and this one has a fierce growl. Consequently, you start to panic, experience nervousness and dread that you will be bitten. Your anxiety is so acute that you cannot stay calm; the fear besieges you. The owner moves away with the dog, but the lasting effects of your encounter will present as neglected trauma.

During panic attacks, your anxiety response will manifest itself in both physiological and psychological ways, as described above. Awareness and understanding are the first steps to breaking your patterns, making better choices and creating lasting change.

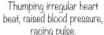

Fight - Flight - Freeze Response

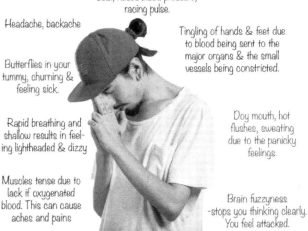

Thumping irregular heart beat, raised blood pressure, racing pulse.

Headache, backache

Butterflies in your tummy, churning & feeling sick.

Rapid breathing and shallow results in feeling lightheaded & dizzy

Muscles tense due to lack if oxygenated blood. This can cause aches and pains

Tingling of hands & feet due to blood being sent to the major organs & the small vessels being constricted.

Dry mouth, hot flushes, sweating due to the panicky feelings.

Brain fuzzyness -stops you thinking clearly. You feel attacked.

Bladder relaxes - feels like you need to go to the toilet & when you get there you cannot.

The Fawn response is more psychological than physiological.

The IMPACT OF THREATS creates a SIMPLE FOCUS

As a result of the development of my learning experience and training, I have created a process called SIMPLE FOCUS to regain control in perceived threatening situations and circumstances.

Self-esteem issues and lack of confidence

Isolation and loneliness

Mental well-being impediment

Physical ill health

Loss of control of your life

Excessive thoughts and behaviours

Most people ignore anxiety until it manifests as a physical symptom, such as cardiac and respiratory problems, pain and digestive issues. For example, you may feel under attack, start to feel breathless, your heart will beat faster, and you will feel shaky, and to overcome the anxiety and panic your behaviour may change. Unresolved tension can also be the cause of unhealthy lifestyle choices, abuse and loss of self-control. Often you will find yourself drinking too much, overeating unhealthy foods and smoking, and even drug abuse. Anxiety is always present in our daily lives. However, it becomes heightened when there is something new, or a transition is about to occur.

When someone experiences anxiety, your first thought may be that 'they are worrying too much'. For most people, anxiety can be invisible to others. However, you might internalise your stress, doubts and worries, resulting in you becoming too scared to show your emotions for fear of judgement. It is time to refocus your thoughts. Instead of focusing on the negativity – 'I feel this task my boss has given me is too difficult' – you can refocus on thinking more positive thoughts, such as, 'Wow, my boss must think I am capable of doing this task; I will have a go.' The human response is usually to rush to the negative thoughts immediately.

❖ You can get anxious more often these days than before, and this has stopped you from being yourself and doing the things you used to.

❖ You want to be less anxious in your daily life.

❖ If you have anxiety, you will tend to hide it from others. You believe it stigmatises you as having 'mental health issues', and that you are unable to cope as well as others.

In modern times, people are ashamed and embarrassed about having anxiety. But admitting that you have it and seeking professional help is not the norm. You will try to push the feelings away too until you reach a point of being in an emotional crisis. You may also tend to withdraw from others or comfort eat socially. Age, gender and employment status are some of the factors that shape people's anxiety experience.

Face your Fear – Say it out loud and proud

Overcome your negativity to build your self-confidence

Communicate about it and do some physical activity

Understand what your triggers are

Strategies – Coping techniques, breathing control and support

Use SIMPLE FOCUS to reframe and create lasting change

How to Break the Cycle of Anxiety

Reframe and create change: When faced with triggers for anxiety and panic, you will be having negative thoughts. The power manifests itself in changing negative thoughts by reframing them with a positive outlook. Therefore, if you reframe your choice, your response will improve the quality of your life. A definite choice will break the circuit and create new neural pathways in your brain. Experience, case studies and theory illustrate that by using tried and tested techniques, skills and tools, you can change your thinking, words and behaviours. Emphatically, to create a different outcome, you MUST do different!

The ABC Method used here as 'Activation – Beliefs – Consequences' is a tool that can awaken your awareness to a situation. When you are conscious of what is happening physiological and psychological, it enables you to find a different way of thinking, taking action and outcome. These alternative ways of thinking will create new neural pathways in the brain. Over time with practice, it will empower you to create a fresh response that is rational and safe. Back in the driving seat, you regain control of a situation and improve your self-esteem, confidence and well-being.

A	B	C
ACTIVATION – Triggering/ incidents, places, people.	Your BELIEFS about what is happening at that moment.	CONSEQUENCES – the outcome of all your negative thoughts, words and actions.
What was occurring in your life that made you feel like this? Where were you, and with whom? What were you doing? When did this start?	What thoughts or images were going through your mind? What did this say or mean to you? What is the worst thing that could happen?	What physical sensations do you feel in your body? What behaviour or actions comes out of this unhelpful thinking? What do you feel like doing due to this unhelpful thinking?
SEE A BULLDOG!	FLASHBACKS, UNHEALTHY MEMORY, I WILL FEEL PHYSICAL PAIN, I MAY HAVE TO GO TO HOSPITAL, NEED INJECTIONS FOR RABIES.	RAPID HEARTBEAT, SWEATING PALMS, TREMBLING, SHORTNESS OF BREATH. Freeze, Avoidance, say something you don't mean. Running away, shouting at the owner, become angry.
NOW IT'S YOUR TURN!		

CASE STUDY

Sheila's Story: Overcoming Anxiety and Fear is possible when you are ready to choose a different outcome.

Problem: Sheila suffered from anxiety when driving long distances, and she panicked at the thought of being in a car for a long time, which then made her feel sick. Her survival response triggered when her husband suggested that they go to the seaside for a day out with the kids. Sheila was excited, but nervous as well. She was too busy to think about it before they left as she prepared a picnic, toys and games for the beach, all the beach stuff; blankets, umbrella and sunblock. Her husband put the address into Google Maps; realising this beach he had chosen was two and a half hours away then triggered her anxiety. Sheila could not cancel the trip as the kids were excited and jumping up and down in the back seat. She started to panic, had fearful thoughts of the car crashing, her being sick in the car. The whirling thoughts sent a signal to her brain of her high anxious state; panic ensued. These thoughts kept going around and round until she insisted her husband stop the car where she was sick at the side of the road.

What we did: Talking Therapy, including the SIMPLE FOCUS Approach. This was a safe and supportive environment that enabled Sheila to express her thoughts and emotions without fear of judgement. By adopting this multisensory approach, Sheila improved her self-awareness. With insight discovered, Sheila was able to focus on the more positive aspects of raising self-esteem. In this happier and more positive state, Sheila had a platform to create possible solutions supported by me.

During discussions, we explored possible new situations and experiences. Next, we collated those plausible and potential situations. We used the ABC chart (Activation – Breath – Consequences) as part of her therapy. After sifting through each of these areas, we were able to pinpoint and identify the cause of the anxiety leading to her panic attacks. Sheila had forgotten a childhood car accident where her mum was severely hurt, and she broke her arm, resulting in her being absent from school for a while. Finally, we used the ABCD chart which enabled her to come up with what she can do differently in the future when she is on a lengthy car journey.

Result: Through the use of the ABCD chart (Activation – Breath – Consequences – Do Different), Sheila was able to use it to desensitise her panic and fear slowly. She understood her triggers and, together with her family, she trialled small car journeys to build her confidence. She learnt to Breathe through her fear and implemented the SIMPLE FOCUS Approach, whereby she was able to mindfully deal with and change her uncomfortable thoughts of doom.

A FRESH PERSPECTIVE

The power of Narrative Questions to create alternative ways of thinking, use of language and acting will dramatically change your life. After all, it is your old perspective that brought you to those dreaded feelings of anxiety and panic. Now, look at the ABCD Chart. We have added the D column, which will help you change your thinking. This allows you to consider what you could do that's different. You can find alternative ways, instead of your usual thinking patterns and behaviour – DO DIFFERENT to create a different outcome.

A	B	C	D
ACTIVATION – Triggering/ incidents, places, people.	Your BELIEFS about what is happening at that moment.	CONSEQUENCES – the outcome of all your negative thoughts, words and actions.	DO DIFFERENT – Take action to create a different outcome.
What was occurring in your life that made you feel like this?

Where were you, and with whom? What were you doing? When did this start? | What thoughts or images were going through your mind?

What did this say or mean to you?

What is the worst thing that could happen? | What physical sensations do you feel in your body?

What behaviour or actions comes out of this unhelpful thinking?

What do you feel like doing due to this unhelpful thinking? | |
| SEE A BULLDOG! | FLASHBACKS, UNHEALTHY MEMORY, I WILL FEEL PHYSICAL PAIN, I MAY HAVE TO GO TO HOSPITAL, NEED INJECTIONS FOR RABIES. | RAPID HEARTBEAT, SWEATING PALMS, TREMBLING, SHORTNESS OF BREATH.

Freeze, Avoidance, say something you don't mean.

Running away, shouting at the owner, become angry. | |
| NOW IT'S YOUR TURN! | | | |

In this exercise, the impact can start with a single trigger or an activating event. Consider whether your anxiety or panic is valid, or whether you have exaggerated it in your mind. Ask yourself, 'What are the benefits of feeling anxious and panicked?' From your responses, you will begin to see more clearly why feeling anxious and panicked is not making you feel happy. You can start to shift your perception.

A question to ask yourself: how INTENSE is anxiety/panic in YOUR current problem?

Moderate   Not intense   Very

How intense is the feeling to change your anxiety and panic to be calm?

What is the likelihood you will act?

◆ PART FOUR: THE ART OF BEING CALM

Three Ways to Feel Calm

1. The Power of Meditation and the Breath

For thousands of years, originating in the East, meditation has been considered a powerful way to take control of your mind. It begins by finding a quiet place to sit upright, eyes closed, and palms facing upwards resting on your lap.

All meditation starts with focusing on your breath – inhalation and exhalation. Concentrating on your breath is the one guaranteed way to quieten your mind and bring your conscious attention to the breath. After all, it is that first breath at birth that gives us life. No matter how many times your mind will try to throw thoughts at you, you learn to simply ignore them by returning attention to the inhale and exhale of the breath.

Like everything new you try, it can be challenging at first. Still, with practise, you can soon master this powerful tool. Find opportunities to explore further the many ways in which meditation can be experienced and support you in developing a calm and controlled mind.

2. Mindfulness

Mindfulness is a practice that brings your attention to your breath and WHAT is happening in the present moment. When you focus on the present moment, you cannot experience anxiety as it is concerned with the future, not depression and sadness, for it resides in the past.

Mindfulness allows you to find the joy, peace and love at the moment with a pure focus on whatever you want to bring to your mind's intention. Use Narrative Questions to explore it in its entirety. The aim is to only focus on that one thing at that moment, such as:

❖ A candle flame

❖ A flower

❖ Drinking a cup of coffee

❖ Cooking a meal

❖ Giving gratitude

3. Nature

It is a well-known fact that when you are stressed, anxious or feeling panicked, walking in nature can soon calm you down. You have to identify which aspect of life brings you the most peace. For some, it will be mountains and lakes, others the sea and perhaps fields and forests. Many people love to garden so they can connect with the earth and appreciate and benefit from the healing properties of grounding in this way.

The ground-ness that it brings, roots you to Mother Earth. In doing so, you can release negative energy and replace it with the positive energy as your feet (preferably bare) connect with the ground. This practice allows the natural flow of energy that benefits your mind and body.

Whenever you can make grounding part of your routine, it will not only balance your energy but build on the strength and power of Mother Nature.

♦ **BOOSTED CONFIDENCE**

While living with anxiety and panic attacks is a terrifying experience, it is not a lifelong burden. Research, information and evidence illustrate that once you awaken your awareness, you can then begin to understand how they impact you, your body and life.

Once armed with this knowledge, you can start to make better and different decisions. You will be able to make choices that create the change you desire so that you can live your life with vitality, calm and happiness.

Seeking support is also a vital strategy that you can use once you understand that change always needs the help of others to move forward. After all, athletes have coaches to help them become better at their chosen sport.

There are also many tools you can use over and over again to keep you healthy. In the process, you build resilience as well, to be able to deal with old emotions and physical symptoms should they dare raise their head again.

Andrea's Learning Alerts to zap your ANXIETY AND PANIC

❖ Anxiety is an activating internal dialogue.

❖ Panic attacks are a mental response on the body to perceived danger.

❖ The Anxiety Loop can be broken with Awareness, Reframe and Doing Different.

❖ Recognising your own patterns of Fight-Flight-Freeze-Fawn responses empowers you.

❖ You can reframe your mind to think differently for a favourable outcome.

❖ You can consciously transform your mind to create positive coping strategies.

❖ Conscious Breathing, Mindfulness and Being in Nature enables you to connect within and be in control of your emotional state.

❖ Ask Narrative Questions on the 1-10 Scale.

CHAPTER THREE
Pent-up Emotions

'Your emotions are the slaves to your thoughts, and you are the slave to your emotions.'

Elizabeth Gilbert
No 1 New York Times best-selling author of
Eat, Pray, Love

Life in the 21st century can be an exaggerated, emotional experience, especially around career choice, money and relationships, because of the pressure put on us to be everything to everyone. Newton's Laws of Emotions suggests that we are the total of our positive and negative emotions.

This aspect of exploring positive and negative emotions is a similar situation to what you read in Chapter One, in the story of the two wolves. Go back and reread it, and see it in this new perspective too. It is a compelling metaphor which is evident in many of life's situations. Knowing and applying the lesson of this story will enable you to make better choices.

You can empower yourself, knowing that your emotions impact your feelings, thoughts and behaviours. Without caution and awareness of this knowledge, you are driven by your subconscious, which in turn brings stress factors, fears and anxiety to your awareness. The more you feed the negative emotions with negative thoughts, the more stressed, anxious and upset you become. You fuel these thoughts and ideas igniting a more powerful feeling. Remember the story of the two wolves.

In general, we can feel deep or light emotions at any moment about anything and everything under the sun. A secret to taking control of your feelings is acknowledging the effect 'positive or negative emotions' have on your mind and body. One questions to ask yourself is if the overthinking of your emotions will cause stress issues or not.

Many people suppress their negative emotions, fearing the judgement of others because of the choices they make. Over time, these emotions, stored in the subconscious mind, will often arise at a time you least expect. You believe facing these dark emotions will only amplify the problem; therefore, you simply and easily bury them and ignore them once again. Remember, if you do not face up to your negative emotions, they will continue to haunt you until you take action to change the feelings into positive ones.

Suppressed emotions often manifest themselves within you in an unconscious manner. As a result, sometimes, when you cannot moderate your emotions, feelings and thoughts, you will attempt to control the feelings of everyone else around you instead. How often have you felt angry about something only to snap at a loved one or colleague because you have not resolved the original issue?

You begin to see the mirror image of what is going on inside you in others. When you choose this path, your pent-up emotional reactions will make you unpleasant to be around, making everyone close by feel uneasy and stressed too. Consider someone you know who is challenging to be around, and you often feel like you are walking on eggshells. At times, this can be you too! When you acknowledge what you are feeling, thinking and how it impacts you, the negative emotions lose power. You will no longer need the external world to provide you with a reason to feel guilty, sad or angry. Empower yourself by taking control and making different choices.

However, you can teach your emotional body how to use fear, anger and sadness to love better, stress less, build courage, manifest joy and forgive more easily. Most of your thoughts and feelings come from your memories, events and situations that you have experienced; both good and bad.

If you think, feel and act in a particular manner, you begin to create a reflective attitude. This attitude is a cycle of short-term thoughts and feelings which you experience over and over again. Think about a recurring problem that you keep churning over and over in your mind. This recycling of old thoughts does not make it go away; instead, it intensifies them. Yet you keep doing it! Ask yourself why. Your negative attitudes are a shortened quality of your experiences. If you string a series of your perspectives together, you create a belief. Many of your negative behaviours result from your limiting beliefs.

Beliefs are any cognitive content held as *exact* cognitive content; the sum or range of perceptions discovered or learned convictions from your past, culture, upbringing, community, politics and religion. No wonder you feel overwhelmed by what you believe. Beliefs created from other people's expectations, which you often live by, are called Limiting Beliefs, because you have not established the belief from your views or experiences. These limiting beliefs are mostly erroneous, keeping you small and preventing you from being who you are truly born to be.

Consider what you believe about money. Perhaps you grew up with little money and heard time and time again, one of your parents say, 'Money doesn't grow on trees!' These attitudes and words impact you as a child and remain with you until you decide one day to do something about it. Over time, these experiences, beliefs and ideas become part of your subconscious mind.

When you add beliefs together, you create a perception which you become aware of, often through your senses. Your emotions are affected when you perceive a scary event, e.g. you see a giant spider walk across the floor in front of you.

If the emotion intensifies and is ignored, you are fuelling your mind and body with stress, anxiety and fear. This everyday event that has elicited a fearful reaction becomes programmed into your subconscious mind: you develop anxiety and a fear of spiders. The resulting behaviour is that you choose to avoid rooms with spider webs due to the programming. Your emotional reaction or action will be to fear all spiders, even the little ones. Over time without breaking this cycle of thinking, feeling and acting, you can seriously find yourself phobic about the subject matter that is magnifying your stress, fear and anxiety.

Paradoxically, sometimes staying in fear is perceived as a better solution to facing your fear. Consequently, you remain with the self-created emotional state, and 'do' whatever the program has taught you from experience, i.e. feel stressed, anxious or fearful. However, if you attempt to ignore the feeling and replace it with an alternative false emotion as a way of continuing to numb it, your rationality will become very fragile.

When you focus on the above negative traits, arguably you cannot divorce the emotion from the thought. That's why people argue vehemently about a situation they consider to be true, despite evidence proving otherwise, e.g. someone may point out that your fear of spiders totally is irrational. You may agree with them deep down, yet you argue that you cannot change how you feel. Your judgement is impeded by this thinking pattern, making it more of a challenge to break.

Stress and the related issues stem from your emotional reactions that have been denied, suppressed, ignored, misunderstood and poorly handled. If your distressing thoughts and feelings, i.e. your emotions, are not addressed in a transformative manner, they can cause a variety of issues. They could range from substance abuse, overeating or drinking, relationship problems, financial mismanagement and poor physical health.

When you can manage your emotions, then you can get a handle on your issues, face them and feel stress-free. These can filter positively into every aspect of your life, through the choices you make every single day.

Everything is a constant change in motion.

**'Nothing stands still;
life changes in the blink of an eye.'**
Andrea Smith

♦ MY STORY

Extended family: When I was a young girl, aged 12, I attended a family gathering. It was a large lunch gathering, and all the extended family were there. Knowing that my immediate family was not wealthy, my aunt came up to me and reminded me to eat a full plate of food. She said that when I go home, there won't be enough of a wide variety of decent food, so it would be better for me to eat the quality food on offer. We were four kids (three sisters and one brother). Feeling insulted, I subconsciously took her words and imprinted them on my mind. I loved my family, but just because we were not well off, this was no reason for people to be rude. So, I decided there and then that I would work hard, study, gain a degree and 'Show them!' I was not going to be the typical kid who gets a job in an office or a call centre. I would make it; by that, I meant a 'decent' job, have a successful career and help my family. I was determined to succeed. I decided that the judgements and limiting beliefs of others that were telling us we were not good enough, were not going to define me.

♦ YOUR TURN

Go to your notebook/workbook. Identify a strong emotion you overcame. Using Narrative Questions – What did you do? How did you feel? Why did things change for you? Journal it out without judgement. Come back after you have completed this activity.

◆ THE POWER OF THE METAPHOR

Two Little Boys

Several summers ago, a teacher was sitting on a sea wall resting after a long hike on the Cornish coastal path. She was eating a sandwich and observing events on the beach. Two young boys, around six years old, were playing together. They ran around for a while, having fun, and now, a little tired from their activities, they sat down near her and began talking.

Perhaps they'd just met, as children quickly do on holiday; at any rate, they seemed engrossed in conversation. Finally, one said to the other, 'What do you want to be when you grow up? I'm going to be a brain surgeon.'

'Gosh, I don't know,' said the other boy. 'I've never thought about it. I'm not very bright, you know.'

The Cornish wind took the rest of their conversation away. And the teacher was left wondering where that second little boy developed his limiting belief about himself. Probably from another teacher or a parent! At the age of six, if he doesn't change that belief, or if someone else doesn't help him to improve it, it will affect the rest of his life. Consequently, the lack of help and support will limit his sense of possibility, holding back his potential.

> Beliefs are not real. They are constructs around which we organise our behaviours. So we each behave as if our views were valid. And for this reason, all our beliefs come true, for theories, (whether empowering or limiting) are self-fulfilling prophecies.

When you consider your limiting beliefs around issues regarding particular subjects and concepts, it is good practice to sit, relax and meditate on your childhood. During your meditation, you can explore where you may have developed your beliefs. When you decide to change, you can reframe your thinking and replace the negative thoughts and views with more enabling positive ones that open the door to opportunities and possibilities.

♦ UNFOLDING PHILOSOPHY

Consider the impact of emotion on your physical and mental well-being, including your choice of lifestyle.

Mental and Emotional refer to two types of human behavioural pattern with both similar and different features of identification. Studies have shown that there is a fantastic relationship between the human mind and emotions we experience in our day to day life. Furthermore, it has been proven that human beings experience both mental and emotional behaviours in different stages of life. However, psychological behaviour is known to be concerned with the human brain, whereas emotional behaviour is concerned with the heart. Mind and heart are the main difference between mental and emotional.

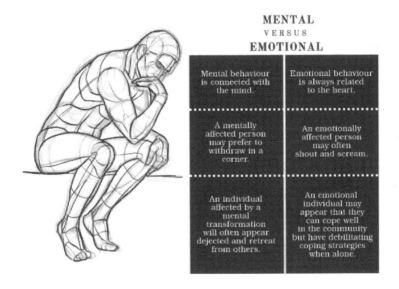

MENTAL
VERSUS
EMOTIONAL

Mental behaviour is connected with the mind.	Emotional behaviour is always related to the heart.
A mentally affected person may prefer to withdraw in a corner.	An emotionally affected person may often shout and scream.
An individual affected by a mental transformation will often appear dejected and retreat from others.	An emotional individual may appear that they can cope well in the community but have debilitating coping strategies when alone.

The importance of the meaning and quality of our existence includes the aspects of our mental health and emotions.

Emotional behaviour almost always deals with the heart. Human beings will tend to show this type of behaviour, mainly in facing adverse life events. Irrational behaviour also has a significant relationship to mental functioning. For example, a person who is suffering from chronic depression might be more drained and have less energy than a typical healthy individual. This physical impact of depression is more evident in a tragic situation, such as the death of a loved one. The brain chemistry and the psychology of mind work astonishingly. They quickly become influenced by positive and negative emotions, unless well controlled.

Various practices like yoga and meditation programs help gain the power and supreme control over the human brain, mind, and its interconnections. These practices are proven to have a powerful positive influence on the impact of emotional, behavioural patterns in your mind.

Emotional stress can also occur when you think that you don't have enough personal resources or experience to meet a challenging event or a situation. Think about flying alone for the first time. If you have a fear of flying, it will heighten with this new experience. In turn, you have yet to gain lessons from flying solo; the experience will strengthen your resolve the next time you fly alone.

The adverse effects of emotional stress cause anxiety and distress as well as an avalanche of physiological responses such as hormonal and cardiological changes.

MentalHelp.net suggests that when your emotional stress is ill-managed, it can take its toll and make you feel stuck. Let's recap on the differences and impact between Emotional and Mental Stress.

♦ THE DIFFERENCE BETWEEN MENTAL AND EMOTIONAL STRESS

MEANING

Mental: Mental behaviour is connected with the mind (or the human brain).

Emotional: Emotional behaviour almost always deals with the heart.

BEHAVIOUR

Mental: A mentally affected person might prefer staying calm and quiet in a corner, which makes it challenging to understand the phase he is going through.

Emotional: An emotionally affected person may produce sounds like wailing and groaning.

HEALTH

Mental: A person with a psychological, behavioural pattern, affected by a spiritual transformation, will often appear unhealthy or abnormal to others around him.

Emotional: An emotional person usually appears as a healthy individual to the community. However, s/he can get back to his/her default irrational behaviour in a second, when his/her mood gets distracted by a certain situations.

To change, you have to understand how negative emotions impact you.

♦ INTRODUCING THE NEGATIVE EMOTIONAL CYCLE

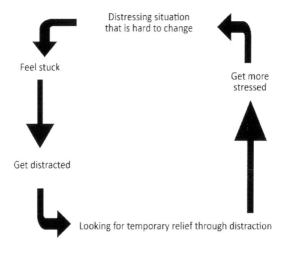

When you find yourself in the Negative Emotional Cycle, it manifests as anger, frustration, depression, anxiety, sadness and grief.

If you feel stuck, you are probably going around in circles and are emotional about the feeling itself.

The feeling of being *stuck* suggests that you are spending most of your time being emotional and hypersensitive to negativity. You only notice the problems, not the solutions. You may talk ceaselessly about the issue and ruminating about what *might* happen.

Consequently, you are living in an incarcerated mind that is trapped in the future and denying yourself the joy of being 'present' at the moment.

STOP! The answer is simple. As the human mind tends to focus on negativity, you will unwittingly create a barrier and find it difficult, removing the ease in which you can consciously change this emotion.

The first step to change is **awareness**. Once you become aware of your negative worry-based thoughts, you can begin to flip these by replacing them with more positive ones. By making a slight adjustment to your current perspective, you can deliberately withdraw your attention from cyclical thoughts about how you dislike your situation. Instead, you can now give your attention to different ideas that produce both a position you want to be in and a better feeling.

The words you use subconsciously describe what you can feel and, therefore, what you can do. If you continue to think about how lost, trapped or stuck you are, then you have no option but to feel those things.

For things to become 'unstuck' of the negative emotion, you have to see them as you want them to be rather than continuing to observe them as you perceive them. Instead, why not use the same amount of energy you expend on worrying about something negative, to imagine how you would prefer that situation to look and feel? You could reframe your thoughts by expressing different words. Think about yourself as being positive, finding another way and free to make a different choice. Consider these words: I am fed up being miserable – I am happy today.

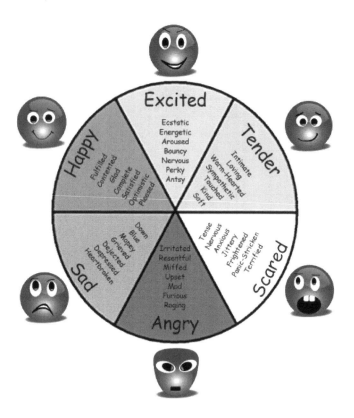

Consider the emotional wheel opposite. Look at the range of emotions you can experience when in a negative and emotional state.

Having a list of each aspect of each emotional state, you are now equipped with positive fuelled words to make better choices for a better feeling.

By taking control of your choices, you can then begin to develop new habits that will improve your mental and physical health.

In Chinese culture, there is a saying for being stuck; it is *'being in the tip of the bull's horn'*. Your calm mind can inhabit the whole bull, but when in a frenzy you are in the dark and connecting to the smallest detail, which is similar to the 'tip of the bull's horn'.

Negative Emotional Cycle

Have you ever worried about meeting new people? Then within your subconscious mind, you awaken a Past Memory. Perhaps the last time you met a new bunch of people, you were at a festival and your sister's friend introduced you to her friends. They were drinking and smoking and did not like you, as it looked as if you were a goody two-shoes as you didn't want to do either of those things. As a result of this experience, your next thought leads you to believe that you will find it difficult to meet new people again. However, you need to remember that you are a likeable person, and it's okay to act differently. The important realisation is that you must be true to yourself.

Emotions: Did you feel terrible last time and don't want it to happen again? It was worrying and stressful, and you did not enjoy that at all.

Physical effects: Your body reflects tension and anxiety; you feel defensive and cannot be open in your interactions with others and feel stuck. You experience further emotional damage. This impact of negative emotions and physical effects reflects in your body language.

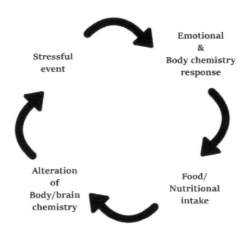

Emotional response: Sometimes, when faced with an emotionally stressful situation, such as a close family member being very ill, you find yourself making choices that you would not ordinarily have to make. If this stressful situation is long or you experience a sudden extra stressful event, such as the person dying, you react from the emotional centre. You disturb the unresolved sensitive areas of your life. You then become 'stuck' in the Negative Emotional Cycle – which results in poor decision-making and being confronted with the fight-flight-freeze response. Consequently, you may lose all sense of reality.

Negative Emotional Impact: Emotional stress can be challenging and painful, and its effects are evident in all areas of your life. It can take a heavy toll and can create a strong emotional response – in relationships, career, daily challenges, and much more.

When engaging in negative coping behaviours, you encounter distress and experience feelings of hopelessness, often thinking you are unable to change the situation. Your body will respond to the way you think, feel and behave, resulting in negative behaviour. Your 'mind and body' reacts, telling you that something is not right.

During negative behavioural patterns, your body releases stress hormones: cortisol and adrenaline. These hormones impact on how your body reacts. In turn, this impact affects aspects of the structure of the nervous system. The stress hormones will also reduce the functioning of your brain cells. You will find that you are overpowered by these stress hormones, which consequently affects the performance of your thinking.

When you are in this negative emotional state, your decision-making skills are significantly impaired; therefore, refrain from making decisions under stress. Your **prefrontal cortex** is the area of the brain that is responsible for decision making, problem solving and paying attention. When under duress, this area shuts down which is why you have great difficulty focusing and completing tasks, even easy ones you are familiar with daily.

In the hippocampus where your long-term memories are stored, it is much easier to forget when under emotional stress, and you may find recall of information difficult.

Have you ever, when under pressure, forgotten how to do the simplest of everyday things, like shopping in the supermarket? I know you often come home and have forgotten to buy the essentials, like milk and bread. The answer is simple because under stress, your cerebellum is affected, causing you to experience difficulties with implicit memories of skills, habits and conditioning.

Under stress, when cooking a family favourite meal, you will find it difficult to remember all of the ingredients. You wonder why the process you use to make the meal and decisions about which utensils to use is complicated. Consequently, the timings become out of sync, you burn part of the food and your usual way of serving the meal is impaired, and it may look more like a dog's dinner.

◆ HOW TO BREAK THE CYCLE OF NEGATIVE EMOTIONS

Think differently

Your brain is like an electrical circuit. To establish a different outcome, you have to pause and interrupt the electrical impulses and create new neural pathways. You have learned that negative thinking gives rise to negative feelings in the body which in turn impact your behaviour. Take anger – your thoughts become irrational, your body heats up, and your heart beats faster. You feel exhausted, shaken and emotionally drained after such an experience. It's time to choose a different thought.

'Holding onto anger is like drinking poison and expecting the other person to die.'
Buddha

Not reacting but responding is the key to creating an alternate course of action

When something upsets you, such as someone doing something of which you disapprove, you automatically react in a default manner according to the programming of your mind. Perhaps you shout, throw things, or even lunge at the person who has upset you. Learning strategies to allow 'breathing space' is imperative to transform your behaviour. Strategies to slow things down, like counting to 10, breathing deeply or walking away, will give you time to calm down, think more rationally and make a better choice. This better choice becomes a response that you have consciously given thought to and allows you to take control of the situation and feel much better within yourself.

Realise and become aware of its instigation and responding

The next time you feel a negative emotion rising within you, become aware of it and label it. By personifying the feeling, you can detach yourself from it and begin to think more rationally. When you are aware, take time to ask why you feel this way.

By connecting within and looking back, you will begin to understand and know what caused this negative emotion in the first place. Once you realise this, you can let the feeling go. Now you can consider an alternative way of dealing with it, knowing you will feel much better by consciously responding and not reacting.

Interrupting falling dominoes

No doubt you will be familiar with the domino effect. Once you tap the first domino to fall, the subsequent dominoes follow on one after the other. It's like a chain reaction. This domino effect is the same for the strategy and default reaction you have to negative emotions and situations. How do you stop it? It's easier than you think – interrupt the falling dominoes. Put in a circuit breaker. Do something different. You have that power to do so. When you catch yourself in your usual destructive pattern, remember the falling dominoes and that you can choose something different to interrupt the chain reaction. That's why if someone is fighting, shouting a different instruction can interrupt what is happening and provide an opportunity to alter the course of the chain reaction.

Uncover new information

When you become aware of what is happening in your mind, words or actions, pause and consider what information you have for your emotional outburst. By thinking differently, you open up an opportunity to uncover new information previously unavailable to you because of your negative emotional state.

The power of repetition

Whatever you plant in your subconscious mind and nourish with repetition, will become your reality (the story of the two wolves, Chapter One). Create new healthy positive patterns of behaviour; choose more empowering, kind words, and learn to be more loving towards yourself.

Fresh perspective

You are the driver of your life, your thoughts, words, emotions, and behaviour. It's time to take control and make choices that take you in the direction of health and happiness, not ill health and stress.

One of the simplest ways to regain control is learning to accept things for what they are without judgement. Consider this – you do not like to be judged by others, then why do you always feel the need to judge yourself, others and situations? Once you begin to accept this as a 'truth', then you can start to understand the need to stop rumination and adopt the Positive SIMPLE FOCUS Approach (Chapter Two).

Putting things into perspective and positive reappraisal, can be learnt by thinking about situations differently. When you adopt new strategies over and over again, they become second nature through practice. For instance, a person who develops anxiety in social situations might require to change the way they think. Take someone who doesn't like parties because of an incident they experienced in the past. They have to shift the lens and find a positive spin about parties so that they see them in a different light and have a different emotional response to them. Once they engage in these new thought patterns, they can change their thinking about parties and, once again, enjoy attending them.

♦ TOOLS TO HELP BREAK THE CYCLE

Mindfulness: A practice of living in the moment. Mindfulness is about becoming aware of what you are doing at a particular time that allows you to observe what is happening, especially in your mind, without judgement.

Distract yourself: A conscious choice to take your focus off what is causing you to feel negative and its impact on your emotional and physical state. Do something different.

Block time off to relax: It is vital to your mental and physical health to create time to do what brings you happiness. It is crucial to find time for you to be you. Do you have a favourite hobby such as art, listening to music, having a massage, taking a long walk or playing a musical instrument? Use whatever you like to do that allows you to switch off.

Emotional Freedom Technique (EFT – Tapping): An energy technique to break negative emotional thought patterns which are attached to the negative energy. When you release the negative energy, replace it with positive thought patterns to induce positive energy resulting in new positive behaviours.

♦ PRESENCE PRACTICE

1. Being present means that you do not revisit the past nor venture into the future. You simply focus on the moment of here and now. Being present enables you to experience the constant awe of the mystery that unfolds moment to moment.

2. To be present, you must be IN THE BODY. However, the mind is continually travelling. To quieten your mind, it has to be present. The aim is a quiet mind in a calm body.

3. Presence Practice will feel annoying, irritating and unsatisfying if you are bored, irritated and frustrated. Presence Practice allows you to choose the feelings you want to feel instead.

4. We can experience poise at the meeting of choice and consequence. Either we choose to ignore this fact, or we submit to it. Honouring is to be present.

5. Only if you can be fully present to what is happening in your life now, will Life's Intelligence reveal itself.

6. To create harmony in yourself, you have to let go of the past and stop fantasising about your future.

7. It is advantageous for your better mental health to engage in Presence Practice. Without developing a sense of being present, you run the risk of becoming desensitised. Desensitising occurs when you fail to be aware of all the subtle information available in your inner and outer environments. During Presence Practice, you will notice sensations in the body, forms of intuitive intelligence, that are extraordinarily accurate and have your highest good at their heart.

8. To be present is to respond to what is arising, moment to moment. When you are continually initiating and controlling, you are nowhere. These thoughts open the door to experiencing emotional turbulence.

9. The more present you are, the more your life deepens, and a sense of wholeness emerges.

10. To be with the present moment gives rise to the opportunity of being open to all eternity as it arises.

CASE STUDY

Problem: Amy came to me to learn how to manage her stress as she was juggling home and work with three young children. She had a nanny at home, but her husband worked long hours too, and she felt pulled in different directions. Work was very stressful, including long hours which were intensified with all of the responsibility she felt at home. Amy had chronic headaches and, due to overeating, had put on excess weight as well as not being able to sleep well at night – typical symptoms of stress.

What we did: Talking Therapy and using a journal enabled Amy to keep track of what were the eight emotions she felt each week. Raising awareness of Amy's stress resulted in her acknowledging behavioural problems. She was fighting with her husband after drinking too much every evening as she was trying to 'wind down'. She recognised how angry and envious she became when she struggled with her emotional stress. Amy had not realised the emotional toll it took on her. When she was in this negative emotional state, it stole her precious energy and time spent with her family.

Some of the conscious states we used were Awareness, Recognition and Acknowledgement. After working through these, she could effectively turn her adverse emotional reactions to positive emotional responses. They included the decision-making process, problem solving and coping strategies to deal with her distressing feelings. Armed with these new tools, Amy was able to label the feelings and emotions, enabling her to feel less distressed. Furthermore, using the SIMPLE FOCUS Approach empowered Amy to feel like she was back in control of her life.

Results: Amy was now able to manage and express her emotions in a controlled manner and recognise her feelings with greater ease. She was able to rationally reason by considering solutions, discussing them and adopting coping behaviours that are more useful and effective in solving problems. Amy felt empowered to deal with future stress and anxiety, as well as being more relaxed, happier and fulfilled with her life.

Consider whether your adverse emotional reactions are valid or whether you have exaggerated it in your mind.

A question to ask yourself: how INTENSE are your adverse emotional reactions in your current situation?

How intense is the impact of your adverse emotional reactions on your mental and physical health?

What is the likelihood you will take action to change?

♦ SUMMARY

Anxiety and stress are part of everyday life but become overwhelming when you place an excessive amount of attention ruminating on your perceived thoughts about a significant matter to you. Becoming aware of the detrimental impact on your mental and physical health is the first step to change, and the desire to do so will allow you to seek new strategies so that you can regain control of your life and improve your levels of happiness. It is possible to turn negative states into positive ones. Once you accept that you CAN do this, you will begin a chain reaction to set down new ways of thinking, talking and behaving, regaining control of your life once more.

Andrea's Learning Alerts

❖ Know the difference between Mental and Emotional Stress.

❖ Reframe impulsive reactions to conscious responses to lessen the effect on your mental and physical well-being.

❖ Adopt a SIMPLE FOCUS Approach.

❖ Step back and detach from the emotion.

❖ Use a Language Reframe.

❖ Engage in Narrative Journaling.

❖ Be Mindful of Presence Practice, including breaking the Negative Emotional Cycle.

❖ Use the 1-10 Scale to determine where you are right now regarding your negative emotional state.

❖ Engage in EFT.

❖ Redo the 1-10 Scale.

❖ Do what you love.

CHAPTER FOUR

Mind Chatter – To Whom Are You Listening?

'The difference between peak performance and poor performance is not intelligence or ability; most often, it's the state that your mind and body are in.'

Tony Robbins
Entrepreneur, philanthropist, and
multi best-selling author of titles including
'Unlimited Power' and 'Awaken the Giant Within'

D o you wish you could stop the thousands of thoughts that go through your mind each day? According to Einstein, we have 60,000 thoughts a day. Of those, 80% are negative, and 95% are the same repetitive thoughts as the day before. These studies expose that the quality of our being rests on the quality of our internal and external communication. No wonder you often feel exhausted, overwhelmed and confused.

Mind chatter is that inner conversation or noise that goes on consistently in your mind and never stops. Some of the internal discussions are loud and clear, while others are in the background. Because your subconscious mind is in charge of firing off random thoughts, you may be unaware that you are doing it. It becomes a deeply embedded habit, from you waking up in the morning until you go to bed at night. One way to describe this inner voice that is chattering away in the background is your 'worry' voice. It appears to analyse something you said or did, or did not do, and regularly goes on and on.

'You are not good at your job and will get fired soon.'

'You are an imposter.'

'You are stupid and are not good at anything.'

'Why are you doing that? What a total idiot.'

Mind chatter is so random that it often does not make any sense. Then over time, mind chatter becomes so ingrained in your mind that it skews your awareness of it. It does not take much to assume limiting beliefs are your truth. We convince ourselves it is true then find false evidence to determine the perception as fact. With such conviction, the people around us think it's real. Do you know that you have scripts you live by, personally and professionally? These scripts, from your parents, friends, colleagues and partners and many more, guide your lives.

Many people, just like you, believe that mind chatter is not something you can control or just stop. Due to the continuous noise over our lifetimes, we develop habits of always fighting within our mind (with little to no outward physical symptoms).

You're either overcome with a sense of **doom**, or feel like your mind and body are fighting each other, and there is nothing you can do about it. When you are in heightened states of fear, anxiety and stress, you struggle just to breathe and get through one more minute; just to push the mind chatter to the back of your mind and ignore the fear to get through the day.

When your mind **replays** the same horrible, negative or fearful thoughts over and over like a merry-go-round, you can't **get off** or escape. Your fear intensifies, you are scared, and your thoughts often become irrational. Despite having a sense of knowing, you cannot get off that proverbial merry-go-around.

Even though you may try and talk yourself out of the fear, it is difficult to stop the negative mind chatter as it comes in waves, hitting you when you least expect it. Before you know it, friends and family begin to think you're 'losing it' because you panic over things which they consider to be trivial. They may even think you are being a 'drama queen' and, even more disturbingly, that you are looking for attention. You find yourself labelled as that anxious person who is always making a mountain out of a molehill. When, in reality, you just want to make it through one more day, and you wonder what it's like to be 'normal' and not have to deal with it every moment of every day of your life.

In today's psychology, mind chatter is called 'monkey mind' referring to your mind being distracted, restless, going round and round; this is your inner critic or voice. It is suggested that it is the part of your brain connected to your ego that's to blame. It prevents you from being creative and doing something you are passionate about and, above all else, being happy.

Kamal Sarma in his book *Mental Resilience: The Power of Clarity* talks about mind chatter concerning mindfulness and meditation. *'I cannot switch off mind chatter enough to meditate or be mindful.'* In essence, this means that when you have your mind chattering in the background, you cannot relax or concentrate.

Relentless mind chatter can be perceived as overthinking, ruminating and sometimes obnoxious, like a rude flatmate in your head, nagging you, irritating you and berating you.

'How awful you are', 'Will my cleaner come in this week;what if they don't?', 'How dare they do this to me? My friends are not nice but why don't they like me?', 'I cannot believe that this is happening to me?' You get the idea.

This mindless chatter can be endless. It makes you sad, angry, anxious, fearful, panicky and restless. You cannot concentrate on anything, and you feel exhausted, and trying to quieten your 'monkey mind' seems impossible. The more you try to focus your mind, the more distracted you become. The mind chatter is all-consuming and controls your thoughts, even though you have the intelligence to know deep down this is not the 'real' you, but despairingly you cannot seem to stop.

'If you know yourself but not the enemy, for every victory gained, you will suffer defeat. If you know the enemy and know yourself, you need not fear the result of a hundred battles.'
Sun Tzu

◆ MY STORY

Choosing to nurse: *When I was 18 years old, I had to decide what subject I would study at university. Becoming a Registered Nurse was my choice. The reason for this was not apparent at first; it was just a strong desire to be a nurse. It felt right for me; it came from deep within. I had a 'calling' and knew that even though there were no nurses in my close circle, I decided that this would be the profession to pursue.*

My dad spoke to me; he told me he felt that I did not have the temperament to be a nurse. Being strong-willed, I refused to listen or be told what to do. In my rebellious youth, I had a quick temper. Still, despite this, I had a sense that being a nurse suited my personality.

As a nurse, you have to be docile, quiet and very much a 'yes' person, with a caring temperament. I stood up for what I believed and told my father that day that I was caring and intensely felt the call of the profession. I innately knew that I would be a great nurse.

I trusted myself and knew what I wanted. With conviction, I believed that I had a calling to be a nurse, and that was what I did. Finding my courage, taking brave and bold action, I defied my family and became a Registered Nurse.

This experience taught me that to be successful, you must have a strong vision, a steadfast belief and steely determination. With these characteristics, you can drive yourself no matter what to achieve your goal and dreams. With these traits, I refused to listen to the obnoxious noises or mind chatter inside my head or outside influences.

'Mind Chatter: a clatter of left-brain storms of stress, overwhelm and guilt along with showers of doubt, shame and fear. Forgive and Reframe the chatter, and clear your mind.'
Andrea Smith

♦ **YOUR TURN**

Go to your notebook/workbook. Identify something negative you continuously repeat in your mind. Forgive it as the irritating neighbour in your head and consider how you may lovingly reframe those words. Journal it out without judgement. Come back after you have completed this activity.

♦ THE POWER OF THE METAPHOR

The Thought Train

Standing on the station platform, sometimes we are advised to stand back as an express train will be passing through at speed. We hear and feel it approaching, thundering through as it buffets us with a strong blast of wind. We don't attempt to jump on the express train and let it take us to destinations we don't want to go to.

We can learn to notice the thoughts and feelings coming, and instead of jumping on that thought train, we can learn to stand on the platform, let it pass, and wait for the right train that will take us to where we want to go.

Metaphors for Therapy

'Most people don't realise that the mind constantly chatters. And yet, that chatter winds up being the force that drives us much of the day in terms of what we do, what we react to, and how we feel.'
Jon Kabat-Zinn
American Professor Emeritus of medicine, best-selling author and founder of the Stress Reduction Clinic and the Center for Mindfulness in Medicine, Health Care, and Society at the University of Massachusetts Medical School

♦ UNFOLDING PHILOSOPHY – MIND CHATTER

What is mind chatter?

Most of the time, your mind is busy with external tasks such as working, chores, hobbies, or listening to music/ TV. When your mind disconnects with the outer functions, it can become immersed in a constant stream of mental 'thought' noise or negative mind chatter. These thoughts can consist of anticipations of future events, daydreams, the music we like, memories, and so on.

Some people believe that they have a better future than others, hold themselves in high regard and think they are in control of the future. However, what they have not accounted for is the 'mental chatter' that is going on in the background, which can have a negative dominance. When you ask someone how they are, they respond, 'I am great, things are amazing'. Deep within themselves, they are pessimistic of their future, self-critical and more fearful than they let on.

Negative mind chatter:

❖ Your thoughts related to inadequacy: 'Sunny will do better than me in the final exams, how will I get into university?'

❖ Your thoughts related to love and positive opinion: 'Greta has a boyfriend – why am I still alone? What is wrong with me?'

❖ Your thoughts related to the loss of control: 'My mum always interferes with my career; how do other people seem to do what they want with their life?'

These thoughts, 'mental mind chatter', are rooted in our principles and ambition, i.e. feelings of inadequacy, love, optimistic opinion and loss of control.

In my training and experience, I have developed a process to identify what your negative mind chatter is saying. You need to ask yourself some of the following questions:

❖ Why do I think that the worse is about to happen? Jumping to conclusions.

❖ Why do I think everyone hates me or they don't like me? Oppressive thoughts.

❖ Why am I using words like 'It never works for me,' drawing generalised conclusions from a specific event?

❖ Why am I always waiting to see if something terrible will happen? Self-fulfilling prophecy.

❖ Why am I focused on the adverse events that have happened? Merry-go-round.

❖ Why am I discounting positive things that are happening right now? Lack of self-worth.

❖ Why am I listening too much to my doubts and fears? Limiting beliefs.

❖ Why am I taking someone else's behaviour too personally? Sensitive thinking.

❖ Why am I using words like 'I should have done this', 'I must be successful'? Self-esteem Issues.

❖ Why am I using sentences that are negative or unbearable, such as 'I cannot stand it'? You have a lack of awareness of the power of words.

♦ HOW DOES MIND CHATTER MANIFEST?

Replaying old stories with the same outcome

Unconsciously, you follow your attention as it moves between negative mind chatter and memories of your senses (sight, sound and smell). For example, as a young person, you witness your neighbour's house burning down. The first thing you are aware of is the stench of smoke, followed by the haunting sirens of the emergency services and then you see your neighbour being pulled from the house. So now, every time you smell smoke, hear a siren or see a firefighter, you are taken back to that frightful scene as a memory. Therefore, each of these elements is a catalyst to something more dramatic than they may be in reality. You remain stuck in the influences of the past.

Truth vs lies

With having 60,000 thoughts each day, holding onto old stories and reinforcing negative thoughts as truth, it is not surprising that you spend so much time in your head. It's not until you have that sinking feeling of 'I don't know what to believe any more' that you find a strength and determination to face what's real and let go of the lies. One question to ask is, why do you want to believe the false-negative thoughts over the positive, helpful thoughts?

Holding on to the lies enslaves you to spend your time on the merry-go-round of trying and not trying to think, feeling doomed, out of control, and not living your life in acceptance, truth and happiness.

Negative vs positive thoughts

Arguably, 80% of your thoughts are negative; that leaves 20% as being useful and positive to living your life well each day. These figures follow the 80/20 Rule, or Pareto Principle, whereby distribution always follows these numbers. If we can intelligently accept this principle as a tool for success, then why do we stay in the 80% negative to 20% positive thoughts? A very thought provoking question. The challenge is to reverse this principle to regain a healthy mind that allows you to live in a state of happiness, fulfilment and peace.

Negative mind chatter cycle

Mind chatter that repeats itself is like a *Tape Recorder* of negative mind chatter playing again and again. This overplaying of the same thoughts digs up the dirt and strengthens the memory of the past negative situations where fears return time and time. Your mind chatter is dwelling on the fears, unable to enjoy your journey. Instead, you engage in the Debate of the Inner Conversation keeping your mind busy, disturbing your peace. By thinking of other things, you deny yourself the pleasure and peace of living in the moment, where true happiness and life takes place.

When you engage in analysing your situation and events, reactions and behaviours from the past, you find yourself experiencing debilitating indecision. Subsequently, that is why you cannot make positive choices that will create lasting change. All of the overthinking and noise leads you straight back to the Tape Recorder of negative thoughts.

Impact of Negative Mind Chatter

The impact of negative mind chatter robs you of living a fulfilled life doing what you love with those that matter. You deny yourself happiness and peace. As a result, you live in a state of stress, overwhelm and fear, creating an exhausted and debilitating version of you. When you are focused on the constant negative mind chatter, you often miss opportunities, due to insufficient attention to what is happening around you. You lack awareness of the world you are living in at that moment.

Your mind is a useful tool, but it also needs to be controlled. Wouldn't it be great if you could achieve a state that's nurtured in positivity? You would be able to solve problems, make significant decisions and, when you're satisfied, switch off your mind and relax.

For example, when you're stressed, you may choose to go for a walk in the woods. The stillness and beauty of your surroundings soon calms you down. It captures your imagination and relaxes you. The same applies to anything you choose to do that you love, such as art, playing an instrument or listening to your favourite music. Extreme sports through distraction quieten the mind, even though you are willing to face danger to achieve the same impact.

Buddhists call the complete focus of a person's attention 'one-pointed', with no time for mind chatter resulting in the 'noise' merely disappearing. *The solution is simply switching the focus of the mind to something you love*.

Break the cycle of negative mind chatter

The most significant step to overcoming negative mind chatter is learning how to raise awareness. It is vital you understand **negative chatter, the triggers, stressors and the impact it has on your life**. One highly useful tool you can adopt when experiencing negative mind chatter is learning how to *release* the negative thoughts and tap into positive ones instead. In all of your conversations with yourself, you need to be able to sit back and find a new perspective. Instead, you choose to review an incident from the past, or perhaps look at your health concerns, leaving you feeling overwhelmed by a sense of gloom and doom. This focus has become a habit that needs to be broken and replaced with new ones.

When you experience a struggle with negative mind chatter, you find yourself in its cycle. You may feel a physical reaction in your body, such as heart palpitations, sweats, aching muscles and headaches, as well as a common avoidance of social situations. Your physical response will undoubtedly lead you to experience an emotional one too. Perhaps you can remember a time when you felt upset, scared, angry, frustrated and thought of yourself as weak. These feelings intensify when you adopt the perception that people are judging you and assume that they are looking down on you. These false impressions result in feeling confused, mental turmoil and limiting beliefs about yourself.

Whatever your past is, you will have begun your adult life with hopes and dreams without expecting the worst case scenario to happen. However, if you have experienced trauma in the past, an element of caution and scepticism creeps in. You become less confident of things working out in your favour. Sometimes you can take it in your stride, sometimes it overwhelms you, and you end up feeling stuck in a dark place for some time. In other words, you feel trapped in this cycle of negativity, notoriously perceived as challenging to break.

Fresh perspective

Waking up in the morning is the optimum place to create the change you desire in your thinking. Once you begin your day with a positive thought, it is easier to create a chain reaction of more positive thoughts. This new perspective will cancel out the opportunity of your pesky negative mind chatter returning. Remember, you have around 60,000 thoughts per day. It's time to take control and choose positive ones for your happiness and more exceptional well-being.

This practice is known as 'reframing' (discussed in more detail in Chapter 5), and it is something you can choose to do when experiencing negative mind chatter. Remember, becoming aware is the first step to creating change. You can stop and focus on what you said and consider how it impacts negatively on your emotions and body. One solution to change its effect is to flip it over and see the sunny side of life instead.

Another excellent method of reframing is to take up the habit of keeping a gratitude journal. Journaling can help you focus on what is working. It enables you to see the positive in your life at any moment in time. Finally, you can take your attention away from thoughts that cause you to feel stressed, overwhelmed or fearful.

Many people today turn to meditation, where you learn to silence the mind and bring to your attention your breath. As your mind begins to respond to meditation, it begins to become less enchanted by all other experiences naturally. One of the aims of meditation is to accept all things positive and negative. This quality state is called 'equanimity'. It allows you to develop a peaceful balance.

Consider whether your negative mind chatter is valid or if you have exaggerated it. Ask yourself what you are getting out of your negative mind chatter.

<u>A question</u> to ask yourself: how INTENSE is your mind chatter in YOUR current problem?

How intense is the negative feeling connected to your negative mind chatter?

What is the likelihood you will take action to change?

♦ TOOLS TO ENABLE YOU TO OVERCOME YOUR NEGATIVE MIND CHATTER

1. **Cognitive Defusion** is a technique that separates or defuses the negative word or phrase as part of the therapeutic process from the emotion-disturbing stimulus. By starting to notice and identify your negative mind chatter, you can positively defuse your word choices by exploring a deeper level of understanding e.g. defuse 'I am such an idiot' to 'I guess I am telling myself I am an idiot because I feel low.' What is it about that situation that makes you feel low and upset? Knowing the cause allows you to make a shift in thinking and choose a more positive outcome with positive language. Now you are ready to use the Negative Mind Chatter Record.

2. **Negative Mind Chatter Record** allows you to focus on one negative mind chatter thought and explore its impact, and offers an opportunity to reframe your thinking and choose a new positive thought.

3. **Mindfulness** is the practice of being and living in the moment as it happens. In other words, you fully appreciate living in the present.

4. **Be Here and Now.** This practice is about focusing on being present, and releasing the demons that belong to the 'irritating neighbour next door'.

5. **Rewriting scripts.** As you see yourself in the mirror several times a day, tell yourself what it is you desire to be and feel: 'I am competent and successful'. Focus on reprogramming your neural pathway and muscle

memory by staying connected to the new positive language.

Negative Mind Chatter Record

0-10: 0 feeling calm and positive - 10 feeling scared and negative

Mind Chatter	Rate these from 0-10	Label or categorise your mind chatter (thoughts)	Negative mind chatter	Challenging the negative mind chatter	New positive mind chatter	Rate these from 0-10
What is your mind chatter saying?		What label (word) would you use for this thought? e.g. 'Oh dear, I feel stupid!'	How does this mind chatter adversely affect/impact you?	Challenge the mind chatter by asking yourself questions that dispute that thought.	Describe an alternative thought that is better for you. Repeat this positive thought 8-10 times with true meaning.	
'I am scared for my life! What if something bad happens to me?'	9	An over-exaggerated thought. It's untrue.	'Oh, my heart is racing, I'm going to have a heart attack. I better not do anything.'	Your heart always races when you are scared. What were you thinking about before your heart started to race? Has anything bad happened before?	It's okay. Take a deep breath. You are safe and well.	4
Your Turn						

CASE STUDY

Brian's Story: Brian is an ex-colleague whom I witnessed having a negative mind chatter episode. He believed he had cancer, even though all his tests had come back negative.

When I questioned him further about why he thought he had cancer, Brian explained that one of his friends received a misdiagnosis. His friend then had a call six months later, and learnt of his end-stage cancer. Recently, Brian said he too was feeling different, unwell, exhausted all of the time. He complained about being achy and he was sure that something was seriously wrong with him. He dismissed his family and friends' diagnosis of depression. Brian was fearful that the GP had got his diagnosis wrong.

The negative mind chatter was causing him stress, anxiety, and fears, which meant that he could not sleep at night, and these reinforced his negative emotions. His actions lead to low self-confidence, low self-esteem and stress. I told him he did not have a definite diagnosis, but he refused to listen and said, 'I am sure it's cancer, I am going to die.'

What we did: To begin with, using Talking Therapy, I identified Brian's negative mind chatter. Once highlighted, we then used the Negative Mind Chatter Record to write down his responses and information. The result of this exercise allowed Brian to see his thoughts in black and white. With this awareness, it allowed him to remove the emotion from the mind chatter. He was then objectively able to find alternative ways of thinking and reframing using positive language. After exploring several tools, Brian chose to use Mindfulness as his preferred method of dealing with his negative mind chatter. He wanted to quieten his mind and stay in the present moment. Brian understood that it was playing the tape recorder of an experience that had a detrimental impact on his health and well-being. Finally, we used Reframe and Rewriting Scripts to lessen the impact of his negative mind chatter, and provide him with an alternative way of dealing with his fear.

Result: Brian was able to let go of his friend's outcome as he realised during his session that he needed to focus on himself. He left feeling calmer and had a range of strategies and tools for his future use, should he require them. Brian felt happier in himself and more confident that he could lead a 'normal' life and enjoy his experiences and family once more.

Changing our behaviour is a process, not an event.

◆ FINAL THOUGHT

When your mind chatter becomes negative, which is about 80% of your thoughts each day, it's time to stop, rethink and take action. Breaking negative mindset chatter cycles and patterns, as well as knowing your triggers, are the key to living a happier and healthier life. Becoming aware of these thoughts is the first step to change. Once you start to notice these, you can implement many tips, techniques and strategies such as Cognitive Defusion, Mindfulness and Rewriting Scripts to reframe, making lasting change to your daily thoughts.

ANDREA'S LEARNING ALERTS

❖ Become 'Aware' of your mind chatter.

❖ Learn how to reframe negative mind chatter using positive language.

❖ Use Cognitive Defusion.

❖ Be aware of the Negative Mind Chatter Record as a tool for change.

❖ Rewrite your life script.

❖ Switch your focus to something you love.

CHAPTER FIVE
Reframe – Regaining control

'Reframing is about creating a new mental landscape with a larger scope of freedom, a greater degree of flexibility, and a set of alternative ways of approaching any problem.'

Avinash Vagh
Student of Philosophy

We all have a faded photograph in an old frame of a young family member who has now left childhood and grown up. It's time to take out the old picture, replace it with a fresh, up-to-date version, and reframe it with a new frame for a whole new perspective.

It's the same with your mind: consider those old limiting beliefs, unhelpful ideas and thoughts keeping you in the negative mind chatter cycle. It's time to make that change. One essential technique you can use each day is 'Reframing': release limiting thoughts and regain control and respond with mastery of your mind.   The purpose of a Reframe is to change or frame a complex set of unquestioned values and beliefs to better self-serving ones that enable you to make better choices. Consequently, there is an implicit change in your viewpoint. Adopting awareness as a result of a Reframe allows listening to mind chatter; changing aspects of the thought; and to step back or disassociate from your viewpoint of any given situation. In other words, you 'look at it another way'. The Reframe takes you away from a false perception that leaves you feeling unhappy, towards creating a new perspective that makes you feel happier.

For example, reframe:

❖ **Negative thoughts to positive thoughts**

❖ **A problematic issue by considering it as an opportunity**

❖ **Something that is against you to a situation that is not for you – 'I can't do this course but can do that one instead'**

❖ **An impossible condition as a learning situation – 'I've lost my job; I can learn new skills'**

❖ **Experiencing unkindness to being misunderstood – 'No one understands me – I will share how I feel'**

The Reframe Funnel

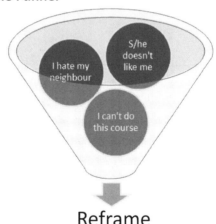

Changing your emotional state of mind by reframing it to a more optimistic and positive state is imperative in regaining control. Consider the following statements. 'The teacher thinks I'm stupid at maths' to 'Let's see what else I can do to change my teacher's opinion of me'. Once you begin to adopt this way of thinking as a new habit, you will start to see many positive changes around you, including the positive way in which people perceive you.

Reframing can challenge your ideas about a superficial longing to be the most beautiful person in the world. Part of the jigsaw is to define what is 'beautiful'. There is an old saying, *Beauty is in the eye of the beholder*. In today's multicultural world, beauty in one culture can be different from another. Therefore, your thought is based on your perception of beauty.

In Korea, women avoid the sun at all costs, as having white skin is a sign of beauty, whereas many Western women favour a suntan.

In Myanmar, visually elongated necks are considered the ultimate symbol of beauty.

Kenyan women of the Maasai tribe are often seen rocking low-maintenance buzz cuts and stretched earlobes.

You can reframe your thoughts in several ways: energetically, mentally, symbolically and physically, resulting in an increase in motivation and success in achieving goals.

❖ **Energetically –** You may be feeling depressed because your husband left you. By reframing your thoughts around this issue in favour of more positive ones, you can choose a new way of thinking that will result in a happier feeling, taking you from a place of darkness to one of light.

❖ **Mentally –** In teaching, when you first learn a new concept, you may not understand it the first time around. The teacher can expand an explanation on the topic to ensure there is understanding.

❖ **Symbolically –** Using analogies and metaphors, a counsellor will reframe, allowing a client to consider a different outcome than the one usually experienced. Using the metaphor of the two wolves, the counsellor can easily show the client that if you continually feed the fear, the outcome will always be the same. But by feeding an alternative positive outcome and taking different action, you can improve your mental well-being and social life.

❖ **Physically –** In the morning, your typical strategy may be to get up, go downstairs, make a cup of tea and sit down and watch the morning news. You may become frustrated at your lack of exercise so a counsellor can begin to explore what you do on awakening each morning. The idea is to reframe your physical strategy to one that includes stretching as you make a cup of tea.

Mark Twain's famous quote, *'My life has been filled with terrible misfortunes, most of which have never happened'* summarises the truth about the way the mind works. Many times you avoid doing the things you like because you freeze by negative thoughts and fears of future events that may or may not happen.

These thoughts give you stomach ache, insomnia, nightmares, and disturb you for a long time. The question is, why do you sidestep changing your thinking? When you do nothing about it, how can you ever relax from those thoughts or have fun?

Reframing can help to explore why you think negatively about the given situation and also support you, replacing those negative thoughts with positive thoughts.

♦ PRINCIPLES OF REFRAMING

When you practice reframing, there are a few basic principles to know and understand that will reveal what is going on in your mind behind the thought.

a. Situations or events do not have a deeper meaning; your emotions, experience and expectations will give you the definition on how you make sense of the occasion. Once you understand this concept, a failure can reveal the beginning of something new.

b. Every positive or negative thought has a hidden meaning or frame behind it, including your underlying assumptions, judgements and beliefs.

c. There is a definite purpose in your negative thoughts. Your conscious mind wants you to change your behaviour, your inner voice or subconscious mind wants you to stay in your comfort zone; a place that you feel safe and secure.

Consider adopting these three principles to reframe your thoughts:

❖ A panic attack may be triggered when you are in a crowded space. You have experienced this previously, so when you go to events with many people, you have a sense of dreaded doom as you believe it will happen again. The feeling of failure is associated with not staying in the room. However, reframing can soon find a new solution, including tips and techniques, that will enable you to let go of the panic and remain at crowded events

❖ 'I did not get the rise because I did not suck up to my boss'; your current frame is that only by sucking up to your boss will you receive a promotion.

❖ 'I enjoy a glass of wine every night of the week.' Your subconscious mind tells you it's okay because you deserve it and need to relax. Consciously, you are aware that consistently drinking every night may lead to dependency. You ignore this thought because the feeling of relaxing and enjoying your glass of wine is more appealing.

'There is no other person on this earth that will better understand why you make the choices you do.'
Andrea Smith

♦   WHEN AND WHY REFRAMING IS ESSENTIAL

Every day, reframing your negative thoughts becomes a habit when you regain control of your choices. You learn the value in rewording and reframing negative or uneasy thoughts by thinking of something more positive. However, there is a caution. If you try to change every idea you had, you will never relax. There are namely three types of negative thoughts:

1. Limiting beliefs that limit you from realising your full potential.

2. When you wish you had more, wanting the wealthy lifestyle some of your friends have and not appreciating what you have

3. Particular problem areas, such trying to lose weight but not being motivated to go to the gym regularly

While it is challenging to reframe every situation and event in your life, reframing can work on most and in turn, make the best of the moments you have.

Here are some easy reframes you can use in your everyday life:

❖ 'I am no good, I am stuck'. Reframe this feeling with 'I am not failing. I am moving forward but in a different direction'. When you do this, you will change your everyday language and words to a more positive one and recognise what words you use to distort your thinking.

❖ 'I am always getting things wrong and never want to talk to her again'. It's your all or nothing thinkings, and needs to be reframed with 'I know she is feeling particularly sensitive and I will be careful next time.'

❖ 'Bad things happen to me sometimes'. It is common to future-think negatively so reframe with 'I know I am going to do well in the future.'

❖ 'Anyone can do what I have done today, and I am nothing special.' Sometimes you minimise your talents, so focus on your strengths and stick to positive thoughts.

**'If you don't like something, change it;
if you can't change it,
change the way you think about it.'**
*Mary Engelbreit
American Artist and Children's Author*

Here is another snippet of my story, where I share with you how you can change the way you see things and reframe it for better outcomes.

I went back to university after my divorce. I completed my second degree in clinical hypnosis (remember, I had a nursing degree already). I was at the stage when my kids were growing up. My son (eldest child) was 18 years old and was doing his A levels. I realised that he would soon go to university and that two years later, my daughter would follow. I would no longer receive any child support from my ex-husband. I needed to be in charge of my destiny and regain control of my life. I had no one I could depend on for financial support. I had to take charge and find my path. I would have an empty nest and could not expect my kids to stay by my side for the rest of their lives. My Masters degree would give me credibility; I would feel great. This achievement would allow me to become financially independent and sustain the lifestyle of my choice. By reframing my state of hopelessness, I was able to choose a more positive emotional state. In this new frame of mind, I was able to create a bright future not only for myself but my kids who can now aspire to bigger and better things. They can see that no matter what challenges life brings, they can set a goal and reframe all of their own and others objections for a better state. This change will empower them to do whatever they want in their lives.

♦ **YOUR TURN**

Go to your notebook/workbook. Identify any negative thoughts you need to overcome and reframe using positive language. Using Narrative Questions – What negative frames have I learnt in the past? How can I change that to make it work for me? Why do I not try this and see how I can make my life better? Journal it out without judgement. Come back after you have completed this activity.

Metaphors are a great way to help you change the perspective you hold in many situations. They enable you to see parallels with your set of assumptions and how your viewpoint may be changed. Know that one idea will have many perspectives depending on who is looking in and what their assumptions are at that time. When you can shift perspective, you can change your beliefs. The power of metaphors is such that it offers a new view for different behaviours and outcomes. Watch out for the light bulb moment.

♦ **THE POWER OF THE METAPHOR**

The Apple Orchard

My father told me that when he was a boy, a woman lived near him on the outskirts of town, and she had an apple orchard. However, she never could get the result she wanted. She pruned the trees right, fed them the way they should be, tried everything. But she never got the big, healthy apples she longed for.

There was always something going wrong. One year, the wind blew the blossoms off the trees, and there was no fruit. The next year, she got a few, but the birds pecked holes in them. Then it rained for months, and the apples rotted. The following year, it was insects. And so on. It seemed she just couldn't get any luck.

She was near despair. One day, an older man came to her door and asked for something. He had a limp, and a twisted back. Life had not treated him kindly, and yet there was an energy about him. She asked him where he was going, and he said 'To the end'. 'Where have you come from?' she asked. And he said, 'We all come from the same place'. She thought his answers were strange.

She then told him about her apple trees and how nothing worked for her. He thought about it for a while and then said, 'Your problems may not be where you think they are. Have you considered whether you are asking the right questions?'

And he went on his way.

It is an alternative way of viewing situations when you do not necessarily look at the literal meaning of the event but instead you turn to question. The next move is to consider a range of questions and not stagnate on a straightforward matter, for it will only give you one answer.

In contrast, when you shift the lens and ask more than one question, it offers the possibility of several solutions. Now isn't that liberating?

♦ UNFOLDING PHILOSOPHY

'Frame of mind' is a term commonly used to describe your cognitive perception or state of mind. While your current mental and emotional state of being is not your whole feeling frame, your subconscious mind holds onto your past experiences, cultures and beliefs. Your subconscious mind is the most crucial part. When you can change the feeling and emotions attached to the frame, you can change the meaning.

All our beliefs come from a myriad of systems such as religious, political and institutional influences, adopting them as the truth. We take these systems, making them into 'frames', to establish 'meanings'. Cultures too represent methods and share ways that make sense of our world. Subsequently, they create models for how we see ourselves and other people. When we were children, we learned frames and meanings of how our society is, or should be, from our parents and extended family. All of the concoction of beliefs often reflect in the differences of opinion with people who have an alternative view from us, sometimes resulting in conflict.

If you do not address your current negative frames, you will continue to live in the negative cycle, causing you to feel unhappy, overwhelmed and stressed. Therefore, it is essential to consider how you may create a pattern interrupt that will enable you to regain control, make better choices and create the life your desire.

STOP doing what you have always done and redirect your thoughts and attention to create new thinking. This will provide better outcomes for your mental health and well-being.

One powerful strategy that you can use time and time again to create the change you need to improve your mindset and actions is Reframing. Simply, take your negative thought, change how you look at it, and come up with an alternative way of thinking.

Reframing is a useful tool used in many situations and circumstances:

❖ when two or more individuals oppose each other

❖ when two or more individuals are in an uncompromising position

❖ when a person holds a negative frame of mind

❖ when a person is negative about everything

❖ when a person sees failure as the end

❖ when a person considers suicide as the only option

Frame of Reference

The Frame of Reference is when your judgement and understanding includes some or all of your perceptual frames – values, principles, culture, religious beliefs, preferences and many more. In using a Frame of Reference, you create meaning to the situation or circumstance. You filter your perceptions through a set of complex assumptions and behaviours based on previous experiences.

In a paper from 1981, Daniel Kahneman and Amos Tversky defined a frame as 'the decision-maker's conception of acts, outcomes, and contingencies associated with a particular choice.' (The Framing of Decisions and the Psychology of Choice, *Science*, 30 Jan 1981: Vol. 211, Issue 4481, pp. 453-458.)

Consider this example. You go for a meal with a friend and then decide to have one last drink at the bar further down the road. On the way, you realise you have to pass a group of young kids with hoodies. Your assumption is, based on what you have seen and heard on the media, that they are thieves looking for trouble, such as stealing from you. You speed up your walking, holding on tight to your friend's hand until you have passed them. As you breathe a sigh of relief, you conclude that they were simply kids 'hanging out' together.

Another example to consider is. Your uncle has a problem with his computer. He struggles as he is not technical and cannot see how to rectify the situation – he looks at his computer as if the toaster broke. You call a professional IT person, and he finds that newly installed programs have interfered with the hard drive. The technician cleans out the computer, so all is well again.

Sometimes you see life as stressful. You often dream of things that are more fabulous than you can have at that moment, such as living in a mansion with luxury cars in the driveway. You may also experience problems that you did not invite into your life, perhaps losing your job. You will say things like, 'Gosh, life is so hard ... is it meant to be this difficult?' or 'I have a curse on me, and hence everything I touch goes wrong'. These thoughts invade your mind and become stuck in the record player until you can listen no more. By making a small shift in your response, you will be astonished at how this one minor seemingly adjustment can create a significant impact. This new way of thinking ignites a new behaviour pattern. Now you can move from the negative frame you are currently holding i.e. that life is difficult, to a different frame. Consequently, it will give you a new lease of life, and invite opportunities as well as expanding your reality.

APPLE AWARENESS – Reframing your thoughts:

❖ Become aware of why you are feeling angry, fearful or negative

❖ Step back or 'zoom out' to gain perspective – re-dress the negative feelings

❖ Speak about it more vulnerably to disarm yourself from the pain and challenge

❖ Identify your negative frame – ask yourself the right questions

❖ Change the narrative and reframe it differently

Awareness

Become 'Aware' of why you are feeling angry, fearful or negative.

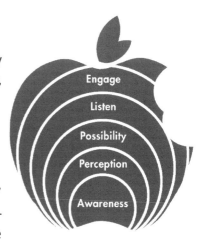

Perception

Step back or 'zoom out' to gain perspective – re-dress the negative feelings.

Possibility

Face your truth and be vulnerable to open up to find new solutions.

Listening

By listening to your inner voice, identify your negative frame; ask yourself the right questions.

Engage reframe

Engage in action by consciously changing the narrative and reframe it differently.

REFRAME CYCLE – To negate the emotional triggers:

1. **Shock Exercise.** When you become aware of negative thoughts, one dynamic way in which you can STOP the train of thought is to shock yourself into being distracted. You could take a cold shower, shout into a cushion, or clap your hands together. Dr Matthew Tull, PhD is a Professor of Psychology, and suggests in one of his articles on PTSD for Verywell Mind that purposeful use of distraction techniques can be of benefit in helping people cope with emotions that are strong and uncomfortable. Therefore, by temporarily distracting yourself, you may give the feeling some time to decrease in intensity, making it easier to manage.

2. **Be Curious** and ask questions. Why do you feel like you do? What triggered your thoughts? What caused the situation to occur? Using Narrative Questions opens your mind to reflecting and searching deeper for answers.

3. **Talk it Out.** Talking Therapy is a psychological tool to support mental and emotional problems like stress, burnout and anxiety. It is crucial, therefore, that you identify someone who you can talk to without fear of judgement. Although you may choose a friend, it is more favourable to find an impartial, trained mentor for this influential role to be optimally effective.

4. **Challenge Negativity.** Setting yourself free from the negative mind chatter is another essential step to challenge your negative frames. It's vital to rebuke them as your truth. You can regain control from being

stuck in those limiting beliefs by moving from your negative state of mind and ask, 'What positive step can I take next?'

5. **See Humour.** Your positive mental health needs to learn not to take yourself so seriously and see the funny side of your negative frame. When you adopt this strategy, you can put the context into a new perspective that sets your free. When you add laughter to the situation, research has revealed evidence that it is the best medicine to change the mental and physical well-being of their patients.

6. **Reframe.** Reframing allows you to look at your situation differently. You can challenge your filters, loosen your keen sense of conviction of the right or wrong way to do things, and consider the alternatives. By finding a new way to look at things and creating new likely meanings, changes in your behaviour will follow i.e. change the frame and change your world.

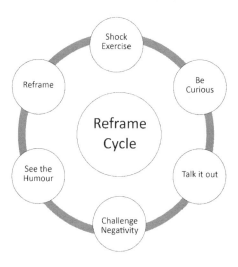

◆ A SUITE OF TOOLS FOR CHANGE

❖ **Reframe Funnel**   to change your self-talk

❖ **Narrative Questioning**   to kick-start new thinking

❖ **Journaling**   to release old thoughts and patterns

❖ **Metaphor Therapy**   to change perspective

❖ **APPLE Awareness**   to reframe your thoughts

❖ **Reframe Cycle**   to change the perception

New perspective

You are hungry for change. Adopting a positive and open mindset is essential to experience success when using any of the Reframe Tools for Change. Without this new way of thinking, you will remain in a dark, limiting world where you continue to struggle day to day with your mental health and well-being.

It is about becoming aware of the words you use, the actions you take and the perceptions you hold about yourself, others and the world. The release you experience when you embrace a positive way of thinking is liberating. You will wonder why you have waited so long to take control and create the life that you only dared to dream.

Once you consciously choose to change your life, you can begin to regain control by reframing your negative thoughts to positive ones using the Suite of Tools for Change. Throughout my experience in life and as a Stress Resilience Coach, I have a firm conviction that every person has within them the capacity to change.

CASE STUDY

Megan's Story and how we worked together illustrates the power of reframing and how it changed her life.

Megan worked for a large American cosmetic company for a long time. She ran the UK office and had a few members of her team who also worked locally to her. Over the last three years, due to the time difference between the USA and the UK, Megan faced challenges. She was sending emails day and night. She perceived comments as personal attacks on her professionalism. Megan's colleagues depended on her, and they also faced similar challenges. Her American bosses did not understand how things worked here in the UK. Megan felt like a pawn and sometimes got caught in the crossfire.

She started to feel anxious and stressed about this ongoing problem. Megan's confidence waned and began to make mistakes, small mistakes at first, and then they grew more prominent. Due to her indecisiveness and hesitation, she lost a big contract. Megan's automatic thought was 'I am worthless, and I will get fired.' These negative thoughts intensified. 'I will not get another job. Who will employ me? How will I manage my finances?' She felt angry, depressed, and her stress and anxiety went through the roof. She was afraid of what her bosses would say and do next.

What we did: Initially, we began using Talking Therapy to establish the situation, how she thought about it and how it was impacting her life. We further discussed her lost contract and her ongoing problems with the company. It became apparent that the company was not a good fit for her. Through these discussions, we gained insight into what challenges she had faced and what kind of company she needed to work for in the future.

Through exploration, Megan realised and identified what skills she needed to upgrade to market herself for a new job. Through narrative journaling, she also considered what career would best fit her skill set. Once Megan understood the need to reframe her thoughts and perceptions, we used several reframing tools such as Reframe Funnel and APPLE. Now Megan could reflect on her present job role, the events and situation she was facing, and the objections she had due to her lack of confidence.

Results: Megan turned her problem job into a new opportunity. By reframing her thoughts to a positive one, she was able to define her CV and job role better, marketing herself as a stand-out candidate and professional. Megan was able to turn hurtful actions caused by her previous company, to improve her understanding of why they adopted their perception. She was able to turn around her perspective of being a victim to a victor. She was able to let go of the anger and need to prove her point of view, allowing her to move forward with strength and conviction.

Megan now has a Suite of Reframing Tools that she can use whenever she finds herself in a similar situation.

Consider whether reframing your negative mind chatter is beneficial? Ask yourself what you are gaining from not reframing your negative mind chatter?

A question to ask yourself: how INTENSE is your mind chatter in YOUR current problem?

How intense is the negative feeling connected to your negative mind chatter?

What is the likelihood you will take action to reframe your negative mind chatter?

♦ FINAL THOUGHT

Reframing is a powerful mindset tool. Learning this vital process will provide 'know-how' skills, whereby you can regain control for lifelong happiness. Adopting APPLE Awareness allows you to see things with a fresh, positive perspective. Your perception of you and the world will change. Using the Reframe Cycle, you can begin to challenge the lifelong limiting beliefs and your bad habits. With the newly gained insight, you can start to shape your perception and continue to regain control of your life. Finally, the Reframe Funnel takes you deeper into understanding the language you use daily. By switching negative words for ones fuelled positively, you reprogramme your mind to work in a way that fosters a healthy mindset and well-being.

Andrea's Learning Alerts

❖ Become aware of your negative thoughts.

❖ Be Curious and ask Narrative Questions.

❖ Challenge the language you use and swap for more positive words.

❖ Don't take yourself too seriously and learn to see the funny side of life.

❖ Choose a strategy from the Suite of Reframing Tools and apply to each situation.

❖ Continue to develop an open, positive and optimistic mindset.

CHAPTER SIX

SOG Awareness – Introducing Stress, Overwhelm and Guilt

'Positive thinking creates another story in our mind. Awareness transcends both positive and negative, allowing us to free our mind.'

Headspace
online healthcare company
specialising in meditation

n today's world, your mental health is as important as your physical health. Generally, to have good mental health is to find ways to think, feel and act in a manner that will suit your needs. If you go through a challenging phase in your life, you will be thinking, feeling and frequently performing in a way that you struggle with and find difficult to cope.

Experiencing mental health issues is not a sign of weakness; it's something we all struggle with from time to time. Throughout your life, you will struggle with feelings of unease (confusion); fear of the unknown (what is happening to me?); and being upset (anxiousness). Your mind will be in turmoil. These experiences will make you feel unwell, and become stressed, overwhelmed and feel less than what you are, causing a sense of guilt as your performance in everything diminishes.

The reinforcement of these negative feelings, aroused by the unrealistic portrayal of mental health issues in TV, film and reality celebrity shows, inflict more of the same on the viewer. The media make light of mental health as they state that 'everyone has these issues'. Consequently, people strive to stay healthy, fight the negative mind chatter and try to overcome them by wishing them away. Adopting this route only compounds mental health problems by not seeking any form of help. It's no surprise that mental health has risen to the top of the public health agenda, as feelings of distress and unease increase, causing isolation from your friends and family.

We all know someone in our lives that have these issues, including ourselves. It can affect people from all walks of life: rich, poor, young, and old. When the stress, overwhelm and guilt consume your life daily, it's time to take action.

♦ INTRODUCING THE STRESS BUCKET FOR UNDERSTANDING MENTAL HEALTH AWARENESS

As it fills up, the stress bucket illustrates how you compound negativity throughout your life. There may be times when you have experienced trauma, and now significant events are buried in your subconscious mind. You know they are there, for they are the moments when something haunting pops up one day without any particular reason. Over the years, without a release valve, your gap between expectation and reality widens, causing your emotional bucket to overflow. During these episodes, you experience a dramatic effect on your body, mind, emotions and behaviour.

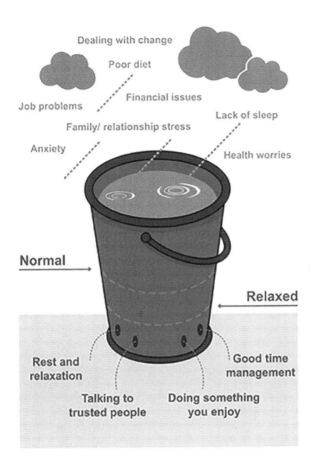

Part of my learning from working with hundreds of clients has enabled me to focus on three of the top issues that people struggle with most in their daily lives. Introducing Stress, Overwhelm and Guilt, which I refer to as SOG Awareness.

♦ STRESS
What is it?

Emotional stress occurs when a gap emerges between your expectations and reality. It can leave you feeling as if you are drowning in the waves of emotion and thoughts that prevent you from feeling happy and living life on your terms. Problems envelop your world, leaving you feeling incompetent and paralysed.

Impact of Stress

Stress manifests in many ways in your mind, body and emotions, all of which impact your behaviour. Physically, you may experience headaches, tight muscles and fatigue. Mentally, your judgement is impaired, and you struggle with simple decisions, and your thinking becomes muddled. Emotionally, you are irritable, apathetic and lose confidence.

All of these and more impact your behaviour and you will find yourself accident-prone and having sleepless nights, with feelings of restlessness.

How to Relieve Stress

Relieving stress is easier than you think if only you open your mind and allow yourself the opportunity. The phrase 'Life is Simple' is liberating when you choose the simple things in life, such as focusing on your breathing, going for a walk and smiling more. Try it; you will be amazed at the result and feel happier.

♦ OVERWHELM

What is it?

Emotional overwhelm entails more than being stressed. By definition, being emotionally overwhelmed means to be entirely submerged by your thoughts and emotions about all of life's current problems. The intensity drives you to the point where you lack efficacy and feel frozen or paralysed. It feels like waves of fear, pain and despair coming at you anytime, day or night.

Impact of Overwhelm

The impact of overwhelm on your physiology makes you respond so strongly to the negative emotion that it releases cortisol, the 'stress hormone'. When you begin to feel overwhelmed, cortisol surges through your body, leaving you overloaded with intense anxiety, helplessness and panic. At the same time, your serotonin stores, the chemical that helps your body fight off depression and anxiety, start to deplete. This combination causes the intense feeling of total despair associated with being overwhelmed. Often, overwhelm is as uncomfortable as it is uncontrollable. It creates physical symptoms such as a quickened heartbeat, perspiration, shortness of breath, or even chest pain.

Overcoming Overwhelm

Overcoming overwhelm requires you to shift the lens and change your perspective. There are three simple steps you can take that will begin a journey to clarity, confidence and calm.

Step 1: Get out of your Head – Journal your thoughts, use bullet points and be aware that this may cause you to feel some hidden emotions. Hang in there as you will learn how to release these too.

Step 2: Change your Perspective – Time to find a trusted person who will provide you with a new viewpoint. The power question to ask yourself is 'Is it true?' Reflect and find evidence of past experiences that illustrate how you dealt with it at that time. Write these down.

Step 3: Take Action – Nothing changes when you stay in your head. It takes action to create a different outcome. What can you let go of, delegate or change that will relieve the pressure?

♦   GUILT
What is guilt?

Guilt is feelings of deserving blame, especially for imagined offences or from a sense of inadequacy. However, not all guilt is harmful. When you do something to offend another person, remorse will usually lead to an apology. Moreover, intense guilt can cause physical symptoms, self-doubt, decreased self-esteem, and shame. It can be challenging to overcome these feelings, especially in the case of chronic guilt. But it is possible to overcome, especially with help.

Impact of Guilt

Guilt is a conditioned emotion. In other words, you learn to feel guilty. Influences of guilt might include culture, family, or religious upbringing. If parents consistently make a child feel guilty or withhold praise, for example, the child may come to think that nothing they do is ever good enough. These invasive thoughts can lead to a guilty complex. Chronic guilt may have a higher risk of depression, anxiety or other mental health concerns.

Overcoming Guilt

To overcome guilt, you have to address the inner turmoil that it creates. Consider the concepts of acceptance, forgiveness and compassion. It's natural to make mistakes, and sometimes these mistakes can hurt others. Whenever possible, attempting to fix the error, or otherwise making amends, may be a good first step. Doing so can reduce feelings of guilt. Here are three more steps you can take to address your guiltiness.

Step 1: Take a Break – Anytime you feel guilty, it's time to take a break. Do something you love, go outdoors in nature; do anything that interrupts your thought patterns.

Step 2: Write a Letter – This activity may be challenging at first, but stick with it. Write a letter to yourself, offering love, acceptance and compassion.

Step 3: Reframe your negative thoughts – Instead of reminding yourself about your mistake and punishing yourself, simply agree that it didn't work out and tell yourself you'll do better next time. Remind yourself about the learning and how it has enabled you to grow by the choices you made. Remember that guilt isn't necessarily a bad thing.

'When you think you can take no more, that's the time to endure one more step, for out of the darkness you emerge victoriously!'
Andrea Smith

As my journey toward discovering how to deal with life's challenges relating to Stress, Overwhelm and Guilt continues below, I will walk you further into my life. There have been numerous ups and downs, and talking about it here has not been easy, but I wanted you to know that I have been where you are right now.

My kids, now adults and spreading their wings, are at university. I started to feel lonely when they left home, so I thought it was time I found a companion. I longed for someone with whom I could share my life. I realised that after spending twelve years alone, I had endured the pressures of being a single mum of two kids, often feeling stressed, overwhelmed and guilty due to the enormity of the task. It was time to consider 'me' and my desires for life. I went back to university to study a Masters in Psychology. There were many sleepless nights, working and studying to allow me to become financially stable. I was feeling guilty, too, because of not thinking about my kids and not taking time out for pleasure. My work-life balance was out of sync. Despite this and being a nurse enabling other people to deal with their issues, I still struggled. However, I understood ignoring my mental health could endanger my physical health too. So I sought help from a coach and mentor to allow me to overcome this part of my life.

♦ YOUR TURN

Go to your notebook/workbook. Identify a problem you overcame. Using Narrative Questions – What did you do? How did you feel? Why did things change for you? Journal it out without judgement. Come back after you have completed this activity.

◆ THE POWER OF THE METAPHOR

No form of physical violence is pleasant. However, when it occurs, there is a fear that it may happen again. When a person becomes aware of a pattern of events, the terror intensifies.

Anxiety identifies past experiences in an attempt to prevent them from happening in the future. As such, the person may begin systematically to avoid any event, interaction, thought or feeling associated with the experience. In this case, the primary function of anxiety is avoidance. When we avoid scary or unpleasant events, the mind can intensify the experience rather than seeing it for what it 'is'.

Anxiety is a way of alerting the body to potential danger or threat, with ancestors and elders referring to fear as a 'gut' feeling or instinct. In today's society, we aren't worried about lions and tigers and bears; we're concerned about bills, work, food, personal/interpersonal relationships, and money.

For those lucky enough not to have experienced severe anxiety, you may ask this question:

> 'Why is it important that non-anxiety sufferers understand anxiety?'

The answer is simple: the anxiety sufferer wishes to engage with friends, family, colleagues and neighbours but struggles, given their fears, worries, and doubts hold them back.

♦ UNFOLDING PHILOSOPHY

In 2018, 74% of adults stated that they were too stressed in their everyday life and were finding it difficult to cope. (www.powerfulmind.co). Stress, overwhelm, and guilt has a huge impact on mental health, and 51% of adults said they struggled with depression, and 61% had severe anxiety. It is very apparent that we collectively need to approach these issues so we can feel mentally healthy proactively.

Stress, overwhelm, and guilt (SOG) are common stress factors, but it does not mean you have to live with it. You must tackle it as soon as you can. SOG occurs when your feelings of overwhelming career out of control. Many stressors impact your mental health and well-being, causing your emotional turmoil. This turmoil can give rise to the feelings of SOG, and there is a surge of cortisol, with intense feelings of anxiety flooding your body. The consequences of your anxious episode result in a depletion of the chemical serotonin, which helps to relieve negative symptoms and increase a feel-good factor. Ignoring your SOG will intensify feelings of despair. When in this state, you feel uncomfortable, and out of control and consequentially you do not know what to do.

Some of the common reactions you may experience are:

❖ You may have an extreme response to insignificant events or situations. For example, you may have a panic attack when you cannot find your keys in your bag, and you worry where you could have dropped them. But in reality, they have fallen through a hole in the lining of your handbag.

❖ You feel extremely tired, ill and helpless and don't know why. For example, your neighbour was a close friend, and now she is not talking to you. You think that you have done something wrong and the overthinking is making you feel ill and tired. You tried to chat, but she walked away, and you are confused about the quality of the friendship.

❖ You feel useless, cannot focus on simple tasks, and your low self-esteem causes you to withdraw from people around you. For example, you had to bake a cake for your sister's 50th birthday, but you felt stressed and overwhelm took over, so you couldn't make it. You previously made beautiful cakes; however, due to your struggles, sometimes you have let the family down. You worry that they will say, 'Here we go again. She is having one of her moods'. These false thoughts will make you feel like you don't matter. So you don't even go to the party and don't take any of the family's phone calls.

❖ Doubt and helplessness manifests in physical symptoms, such as shortness of breath, rapid heart rate and sweating.

❖ Your perception of the world you live in is blurred by the emotional turmoil you experience after being let down by your family.

While there is no way to determine what life has in store at any given moment, there are ways to build up the mental strength to face life's challenges and build resiliency. When you take time to learn what triggers stress and anxious thoughts, you can better manage overwhelming experiences before they occur. With the rigorous application and right tools, you can help minimise the occurrence and impact of becoming stressed and overwhelmed.

Stress resilience is like a magic potion. It's about taking control of your life despite all the challenges it brings. Being resilient creates the 'bouncebackability' essential for robust mental health and well-being.

It is time to become resilient.

CASE STUDY

Maria's Story: After Maria and her husband were involved in a car accident, she sought help. She was stressed all the time; worry and anxiety were her significant issues. Maria recovered fully from the accident, but her husband's recovery was slow. She worried about their finances, mental health, stress and the overwhelming burden she felt with the responsibility on her shoulders. Maria had to look after the home, her husband and the kids as well as work to bring in money. She felt exhausted and lacked concentration or focus on simple tasks. The combination of Maria's and her husband's responsibilities finally took its toll on her. Sometimes during evenings and at weekends, she had to take her husband to his hospital appointments and check-ups. A torrent of thoughts raged through her mind.

What if her husband did not come through his physical problems? How would they survive without a second income? Unintentionally, her husband's family sought information about his recovery and well-being. However, Maria's perception was that they were blaming her for the accident and making her feel guilty for his slow recovery. Regular requests from the extended family for updates, compounded with their advice, made her feel uneasy about her job and her inability to be by his side 24/7.

What we did: Talking Therapy revealed to Maria what was causing her stress and overwhelm. Furthermore, the revelations enabled her to gain insight into her emotional struggles and how much she did at home and work. Maria found time and space to accept that she was the only supporting member of the family now. Both Maria and I acknowledged that she would not be able to feel free from the stress and worry as it helped her develop coping strategies. The change in perception and understanding meant that she did not withdraw from her extended family. With the clarity of mind, Maria improved her assertiveness and suggested the family take their turn in helping her to cope better; to have time for her.

Finding tools and techniques that worked for her, Maria wrote of her struggles in a daily journal. Consequently, to write her thoughts and fears, she was able to gain perspective on how unique her situation was and how her husband's health would only improve.

Results: Maria learned how to verbalise her emotional struggles. She learnt positive coping strategies, and her feelings and mood vastly improved. Maria is now able to take control of her own emotions and use the powerful tool she learned as part of her healing journey.

Narrative Questioning is a powerful tool used along with the 1-10 Scale, to use as soon as you become aware, then use a tool or technique after which redo the 1-10 Scale.

A question to ask yourself: how INTENSE is your SOG in YOUR life right now?

How intense is the feeling rational or reasonable with your negative perception?

What is the likelihood you will take action to change – be constructive?

1	2	3	4	5	6	7	8	9	10

◆ FINAL THOUGHTS

SOG Awareness is the first step to understanding and overcoming your stress, overwhelm and guilt, so you can take action to control it. All of these issues are intermingled and not experienced in an isolated way. By understanding how the 'Stress Bucket' builds up negative emotions, you take simple steps to release negative emotions and relieve your symptoms. Making these steps part of your daily routine will enable you to manage your emotional responses to situations. Over time, the perception of yourself and the world changes, and your confidence grows, allowing you to live your life in a happier state and on your terms.

Andrea's Learning Alerts – SOG AWARENESS

❖ Become aware when you feel stressed, overwhelmed or guilty.

❖ Remember to breathe to create space and time.

❖ Develop a routine to include Meditation, Mindfulness and 'me' time.

❖ Practice reflection using the 1-10 Scale – take a reading as soon as you are aware, use one of the tools and techniques, then redo the 1-10 Scale.

❖ Write down your feelings and allow them to leave your mind and body. You can either journal or write them on a piece of paper and burn it or rip it up. This ritual symbolises letting go.

❖ Find a mentor, coach or therapist.

CHAPTER SEVEN
Stress

'It's not stress that kills us; it is our reaction to it.'

Hans Selye
Hungarian-Canadian endocrinologist,
founder of The Stress Theory and author

Stress, often described as an unmanageable amount of worry, anxiety, fear, overwhelm, and coping capacity, is prevalent in today's world. One of the leading indicators of stress is the way your body responds to the immense pressures of daily life, events or situations. These situations can be a struggle and often cause much pain. You may react to stress very differently from your family or friends. Although stress affects many people from different walks of life, age groups and gender, experts claim that socio-economic situations may intensify stress factors. If you have ever suffered from stress, you may recognise that it threatens your sense of self, and severe stress can cause both short-term and long-term health problems.

An online poll taken for mentalhealth.org.uk by YouGov, one of the most extensive research studies to highlight the stress levels in the UK, has found that roughly about 74% of people struggle with stress and overwhelm and are unable to cope with everyday life. Of these, 30% are from the older generation of the population. Women tend to struggle with stress more than men. However, in today's technological world infused with outside influences and pressures, kids and teens also struggle with immense stress and anxiety.

Some of the most common causes that can lead to stress are:

❖ Divorce or separation from your partner

❖ Death of a family member or close friend

❖ Long-term ill health

❖ Debt

❖ Starting a new job or getting a promotion with expectations that overwhelm you

❖ Moving house

❖ Financial problems

❖ Losing your job

When you feel stressed, your fight-flight-freeze-fawn response is triggered, which in turn activates your immune system. The response will occur if your mind and body feel it's in danger.

However, looking at the other side of the coin, a small amount of stress is beneficial to enhancing performance, creativity and *joie de vivre*. Under such manageable pressure, the body's natural reaction causes a rush of adrenaline, tingling, and a feeling of breathlessness. After such a short episode, you return to a resting state without any adverse effects on your health and well-being. The cautionary note here, however, is if you do not treat or manage stress, over time it may impact you mentally, physically, emotionally, and socially.

Brit performer Jesy Nelson from Little Mix revealed how she suffered stress and its impact on her physically. 'I lost my hair – alopecia – when I was 13 years old. I was bullied at school, and the stress was overwhelming. I am okay now and love my hair!'

During the height of her fame, catwalk model Cara Delevingne had itchy, flaky skin triggered by her stress, a skin condition called psoriasis. She revealed 'people would not go near me or touch my hand as they thought I had leprosy. I was in my fight and flight response for months on end. I hated the way I looked, and it went on for a long time.'

Hollywood actress Emma Stone said, 'I struggled with stress acne when I was 20 years old. Everyone thinks that celebrities don't have any problems. But for my headshots to get into movies, they airbrushed out my facial defects.'

While many psychologists acknowledge that some stress can be useful for you, for others it creates long-term effects. If you are not one of those people who can cope with your stress effectively, here are some of the signs and symptoms you may recognise.

◆ SOME SIGNS AND SYMPTOMS THAT SUGGEST YOU ARE SUFFERING FROM STRESS

Physical changes: When you are struggling with stress long-term, you will feel nauseous, have stomach aches, headaches, and many other physical symptoms. Breathlessness is a common symptom, too, with rapid heart rate, aches, pains, and intense sweating. You may develop Irritable Bowel Syndrome (IBS) or perhaps more severe cardiac issues. You will find it difficult to sleep, as well as struggle to remember things.

Emotional changes: Stress will make you hold on to your emotions (pent-up emotions), fear, and anxiety, causing you to panic about little things or nothing. Overthinking about things may catapult you more profoundly into darkness, and before you know it depression creeps up on you. Many people express their loss of appetite, or conversely resort to overeating and often imprison themselves in their homes.

Behavioural changes: When you are stressed, everyday decisions become impossible. You find yourself feeling irritable, angry and tearful. To overcome them, you may smoke, drink excessively, and sometimes take drugs to numb out the pain.

Social changes: 37% of adults who have reported stress feel lonely. Of this, 16% may resort to self-harm, and 32% say they have suicidal thoughts and feelings. It is often described that long-term stress causes a significant change in personality. You may know someone who once was an outgoing, fun-loving person and today is a shadow of themselves. They turn down social invites, withdraw from family and friends, and isolate themselves at work and home. Research carried out by the Journal of Research In Personality in 2016 indicated that people who suffer from long-term stress change their perception, resulting in them adopting a more pessimistic outlook on life.

'Today I refuse to get stressed out about things I cannot change or control.'
Andrea Smith

Out of control stress invades your everyday thoughts, feelings and life, creating a world of turmoil. When the tension reaches a paralysing heightened state, it impacts you on many levels including mentally, physically, emotionally, and socially, leading to unacceptable behaviour.

Be cautious and do not let yourself get stretched too thin. Learn to say 'no' without feeling guilty. It is also important that you set reasonable limits and clear boundaries.

Elastic can be likened to stress, and you need some pressure in your life to feel excitement and alive, otherwise, like a floppy rubber band, you will feel disconnected and useless.

But remember if you stretch too much, you could snap.

Simple metaphors can help you change your perspective on areas of your life that are causing you pain, discomfort and stress. Working from the inside out will also allow you to change how you look at things, and you can see in one light bulb moment how your perception changes. Now isn't that rewarding?

> *My Story: I would like to walk you further through my journey. At one point in my life, as a single mum, I was working two jobs because I needed money to bring up my two children and survive. During this time, I became stressed and exhausted. With a weakened immune system, I caught a flu virus finding myself in bed, unable to move, let alone work or look after my children. My stress was exacerbated further impeding my recovery time. I was wiped out physically and emotionally. My behaviour changed as I was irritable, short-tempered and fearful of how I would cope if my health did not improve. The first step to my recovery was to ask for help with some of my chores. My friend stepped in and relieved my worry. Once I had taken positive steps to lessen my stress, things improved.*

♦ YOUR TURN

Go to your notebook/workbook. Identify a problem you overcame. Using Narrative Questions – What did you do? How did you feel? Why did things change for you? Journal it out without judgement. Come back after you have completed this activity.

Your body responds to life's daily challenges by manifesting feelings of stress, such as headaches, palpitations and sweating. Stress does not always arise from current experiences. It can creep up on you when your subconscious mind brings to your attention something that happened in the past that you have deeply buried because of the pain. Whether situations are current or in the past, stress can be triggered by simple everyday experiences. You may be travelling to work during the rush hour or adapting to life after a divorce, sexual abuse, physical abuse, or death of a loved one. In reality, there is no avoiding stress. Your goal is not to eliminate stress, but manage it. One individual's stress triggers are not the same as another person's. A range of events will cause anxiety, and if not managed effectively, it can lead to burnout.

Your job in the city is putting more and more pressure on you in this ever-changing environment. Without adopting and taking positive steps, you are soon overwhelmed and unable to cope. When you feel out of control, your self-perception is clouded, and your judgement of situations becomes suspicious. When the boss is looking at you, your negative mind chatter is out of control, and you consider her impression of you is that you cannot do the job. Without addressing your mind chatter and shifting the lens, you continue to see things from a negative perspective and consequently suffer burnout.

Burnout is described as a state of emotional, physical, and mental exhaustion caused by excessive and prolonged stress. It occurs when you feel overwhelmed, emotionally drained, and unable to meet constant demands. In today's modern society, many women are driven to have it all – profession, house, car, holiday, family, children. Many realise that this ambition is not sustainable over time. One way to invest in your worth and well-being is building into your daily routine 'me time' to relieve pressure from the multitasking mode. 'Me time' is likened to the valve on a pressure cooker; you must ensure it can let off steam or otherwise you will be left with a soggy mess as it explodes. Without a release, you experience burnout.

CASE STUDY

Aria's story: Aria is a young Spanish girl who struggled to find work for a long time when she had moved to the UK, as she spoke inadequate English. Aria's first job was a housekeeper, and she joined some local groups to improve her English. She had not been in a relationship for a long time, and feeling stressed and struggling to settle in was one of her daily challenges. Aria eventually found her feet, some friends and started a new job in an office. One of her colleagues at work introduced her to 'a nice guy', and they began to go out. Aria felt excited, but her negative mind chatter led her to feel stressed even when they were together. The negative thoughts, pent-up emotion and stress were making her feel physically nauseous, have headaches, aches and pains, and panic attacks that interfered with the relationship. Aria started to feel anxious, depressed and sometimes would even withdraw, then the stress and panic attacks intensified. All of these factors became challenging for the relationship, and her boyfriend dumped her.

What we did: Aria and I discussed her stressful episodes through Talking Therapy. We used EFT to scale back the intensity of the feeling, using the 1-10 Scale (10 being intense stress and 1 being manageable stress) as well as learn how to use it as a daily strategy to manage her anxiety. Coaching using several techniques such as Narrative Questioning, to gain insight, change her perception and enable Aria to recognise her solutions.

Results: Aria was able to recognise her stress triggers and respond calmly rather than allowing them to cause her usual adverse reaction. She was able to change her perspective of others and understood that the language barrier affected her understanding of situations. Aria regularly used the 1-10 Scale to provide more time to consider the circumstances, adopt her preferred strategy and respond more positively to the trigger. Aria was happier, making new friends and becoming more proficient in English, enabling her to move forward with life.

♦ **TOOLS AND TECHNIQUES TO BEAT STRESS AND BURNOUT**

Three R Technique		
Recognise	**Reverse**	**Resilience**

The Three R Technique is an effective strategy to adopt and manage stress burnout. It includes:

1. **Recognise** – The key to managing burnout is early awareness, so make sure you assess yourself regularly regarding the warning signs of tiredness and exhaustion.

2. **Reverse** – After recognising that you are experiencing burnout, immediately seek the help to assist you in undoing the effects of burnout and manage the stress you have encountered.

3. **Resilience** – Using the metaphor of the elastic band, you have to adopt effective management of your stress. To do this, you must use all of the tips, techniques and strategies you are learning. Use them to regain control so you can bounce back with less emotional, physical, mental and social impact.

Emotional Freedom Technique (EFT) – EFT is growing in popularity as a useful tool for rapid results when dealing with stress, blocked energy and a shift in mindset. Similar to acupuncture, EFT focuses on the meridian point — or energy hot spots — to restore balance to your body's energy. It's believed that restoring this energy balance can relieve the symptoms that a negative experience or emotion may have caused.

Systemic Coaching allows clients, through a multisensory approach, to gain insight, change the perception of the problem, and disentangle all of the elements. With greater clarity, you can create a transformational solution to your challenges.

❖ Step 1: Identifying by bringing awareness and focus on challenges and issues.

❖ Step 2: Mapping as 'stress checker' for situation/ challenges faced, to bring into awareness the deeper issues.

❖ Step 3: Information gathering concerning blocks/ limitations caused to hidden loyalties to people or events in the past. They are building functional interpersonal relationships – by integrating inner and outer past strategies.

❖ Step 4: Feedback revealed through intuition and insightful observation of the process and simplification of a Systemic Coaching involvement to reveal hidden relationship building blocks.

❖ Step 5: Creating Resilience through better choices, clarity of situation, and understanding for effectively dealing with stress issues.

♦ **FINAL THOUGHTS**

While stress is a significant mental health issue in today's society, there are many solutions to it once you raise your awareness. Without taking action to address stress, you will continue to suffer emotionally, physically, mentally, and socially. In the long term, emotional burnout ensues. Admitting that you are stressed and seeking help is a positive step. A helping hand and guidance allows you to learn how to cope with current and future stressful situations, enabling you to live your life on your terms.

Narrative Questioning is a powerful tool used along with the 1-10 Scale, to use as soon as you become aware, then use a tool or technique before redoing the 1-10 Scale.

<u>**A question**</u> to ask yourself: how INTENSE is your stress in YOUR current problem?

How intense are the feelings, physical symptoms and behaviours associated with your stress?

What is the likelihood you will take action to address your stress and change?

```
1    2    3    4    5    6    7    8    9    10
|    |    |    |    |    |    |    |    |    |
```

Andrea's Learning Alerts

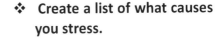

❖ Create a list of what causes you stress.

❖ Use metaphor to help shift your perception.

❖ Journal your experiences.

❖ Use the Three R Technique.

❖ EFT – Releases your blocked energy and shifts your mindset.

❖ Practice Mindfulness at least once each day.

❖ Find a mentor, coach, or therapist.

❖ Use the 1-10 Scale before each technique you use then redo to help you notice the change.

CHAPTER EIGHT
Overwhelm

'Don't let the entire staircase overwhelm you. Just focus on that first step.'

Anon

Emotional overwhelm is when you bury or drown beneath a huge mass of everyday situations and tasks affecting your emotional mental health and well-being.

E motional overwhelm is all too common in today's busy, must-have-it-all world. Without an escape, the pressure becomes overwhelming, and something has to give. Emotional overwhelm is a state where you are overrun by extreme challenging to manage emotions. In a state of overwhelm, before long it affects your ability to think, feel and act rationally, preventing you from carrying out daily tasks.

Without intervention, negative emotions give rise to fear, prolonged stress, or severe illness and financial worries. Being emotionally overwhelmed does not just affect you when there is something significant going on in your life but can subtly creep up on you. This is evident when you take on more and more responsibilities. At other times, you may not pinpoint the cause when you are consumed by emotional overwhelm. It's about being aware of the danger signals that can help your emotional overwhelm tip you over to total burnout.

The UK Mental Health Foundation says, 'Millions of us around the UK are experiencing high levels of stress and overwhelm, it is damaging our health. Overwhelm and stress are one of the great public health challenges of our time, and still not being taken as seriously as physical health concerns.' www.mentalhealth.org.uk

◆ CAUSES OF EMOTIONAL OVERWHELM

❖ **Fear of adverse outcomes:** Your overwhelm triggers may be a particular event, and sometimes they can be multiple situations. For example, you may lose your mum and dad in the same month and with a gap of a couple of weeks. You have not had time to process the first loss, and then the second one may occur. You are now triggered by hearing about a family or friend being seriously ill, and you are emotionally overwhelmed by the thought of a near-death situation.

❖ **Uncertainty and not having answers to tough questions:** You have restless thoughts about your work. For some time, you have been considering starting your own business as you no longer have a sense of fulfilment in your current workplace. You are thinking about asking your partner to support you during the transition from paid work to making your own money in a self-employed environment. You feel uncertain as to how your partner will receive your idea. Consequently, you begin to make up stories of how that conversation will ensue. The ripple effect is that you procrastinate, feel out of control and unhappy, leading to emotional overwhelm.

❖ **Your mind is racing with many thoughts.** You are feeling proud of achieving your long-awaited degree. You have done a few voluntary jobs while you decide on the next step of your career. You have applied for several jobs, but you cannot find the right one to fit your training. As time goes on, you feel frustrated and angry leading to anxiety and depression. When emotional overwhelm intensifies, more robust emotional responses affect your behaviour. You may find yourself becoming angry at unnecessary things: conflicting feelings arise. You fail to understand how you are unable to get the managers to see what a fantastic person you are and what an asset you would be to their company. You are at home all the time now. You feel overwhelmed by the family pressure to get this job, and you feel such a failure now. The joy at attaining your degree has faded.

When there are too many thoughts swimming around in your head, their meanings lack clarity. As humans, we love stories, yet you often choose to tell yourself harmful and hurtful stories that are not true. They are fused with our skewed perception of self, events and circumstances. It is a well-known fact that the human mind will seek negativity rather than a more favourable positive outcome to situations.

A culmination of these negative thoughts begins to overwhelm your being as you start to see the lack of accomplishment. A dark cloud descends, and you feel like you are on the never-ending merry-go-round. Signals of mental, emotional, and physical unease and distress, make you aware and realise that you are struggling with emotional overwhelm. However, you are involved in what is going on externally, that you simply overlook what is going on inside.

'Thoughts of uncontrollability or unpredictability are the backbone of overwhelming,' according to Dr L. Kevin Chapman, PhD, Founder and Director of the Kentucky Center for Anxiety and Related Disorders. 'It is your unrealistic and unreasonable thoughts that spark your stress overwhelm.'

Being an artist, a politician or an inventor comes with inevitable moments of overwhelm, stress and anxiety. There are daily stressors triggered by deadlines, creative blocks and studio mishaps. Those are emphasised by overarching personal and professional concerns related to renting, relationship issues, and getting the next pay cheque on time. These can be some of the broad sources of unease that affect us all, like the political climate and, generally, *the future*.

These are some of the things people say to help themselves:

❖ I find that when I start feeling overwhelmed, it's imperative to step away from it.

❖ I try to suss out which it is in any particular situation. And then I either rest or push myself through the fear of failure or whatever I'm scared of.

The former Shadow Home Secretary Diane Abbott MP was struggling with diabetes and overwhelm during the June

2017 election and had to take some time off. She revealed her diabetes was out of control and was forced to take a break from front line politics to look after herself and have some 'me time'.

'Sometimes finding the answer sounds super easy but it's essential to take a break, breathe and step back from the situation.'
Andrea Smith

Many people have a desire to be busy, not knowing how or when to switch off, step back, or let go of situations. No matter what your profession or career is, troubling circumstances and external events will always be part of life. Chances are that you are familiar with feeling a little overwhelmed, defeated and deflated at some stage. Yet you can feel alone and threadbare. Questions you will ask yourself may include: 'What is wrong with me? Why can I not hack the pressure? Can I push through and brush the feelings of overwhelm, anxiety and stress under the carpet? Why can I not pep-up and work harder?' Your nemesis is not what's going on around you but your own psychological and self-perception.

Sometimes internal pressure to be perfect and external pressure to perform at a certain level will conceal that you are struggling at the moment. You will keep the high energy on repeat and not skip a beat to reveal that it's all become too much, try to deliver the supposed output, and not show that you are failing. The outcome will be overwhelm taking over – time to look inside to find the answer.

◆ THE POWER OF THE METAPHOR

The River

Sometimes you may feel as if you are carried downstream by the current. You struggle to stay afloat amongst the undergrowth, surface rubbish and the filth. See these ugly barriers as thoughts, feelings, events and bodily sensations. The river is your distress as you float helplessly downstream. You have a choice. You can watch from the river bank as the thoughts, events, sensations and feelings drift by you. You can focus on individual items – a thought as a feather, a sensation as a ripple and an event as a stick. You can continue to struggle. The answer is to stand and be the spectator simply.

My mum and dad live in India. My dad had been ill and was physically failing for a while. He had some underlying medical issues that could not be resolved. He passed away, and I went home to help my mum to deal with the funeral and estate. She too was looking frail and frightened. My mum had a knee replacement a few years ago and, unknown to me or my siblings, the same knee was starting to deform. I had a short time to attend my dad's funeral, and then I had to come back to the UK as my kids were being looked after by a friend. I also had to return to work. Knowing that the time I had with my mum was limited, my mind started to do somersaults. I felt torn between wanting to stay with her and being back with my kids. My overwhelm, panic and anxiety only eased when I had a frank conversation with my brother who took time off work so he could stay and look after mum.

♦ YOUR TURN

Go to your notebook/workbook. Identify an overwhelming problem you overcame. Using Narrative Questions – What did you do? How did you feel? Why did things change for you? Journal it out without judgement. Come back after you have completed this activity.

Emotional overwhelm feels like a twenty foot wave repeatedly crashing onto you. Psychologist Marla W. Deibler, PsyD, the Founder and Executive Director of The Center for Emotional Health of Greater Philadelphia, described overwhelm as 'feeling completely overcome in mind or emotion.' When you are unable to manage your triggers, the feelings of overwhelm returns, and it comes in many forms. It manifests as anxiety, irritability, negative mind chatter, and can often lead to a panic attack.

◆ THE CYCLE OF EMOTIONAL OVERWHELM WAVE

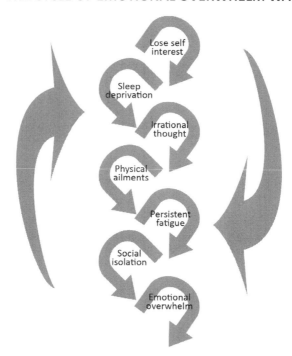

You overeat or skip meals. You are not taking good care of yourself. You struggle to sleep at night. These negligent actions compound and will make you lose your ability to think rationally. The ripple effect makes it even more challenging to deal with the overwhelm.

Before you know it, you are dealing with physical health problems, persistent fatigue and never-ending negative emotions. Over time, without intervention, it can lead to falling ill, and you may struggle to fight infection. The ensuing impact is that your social life becomes non-existent. Feeling caged, you become irritable, lash out at your family, or give in and totally isolate yourself.

CASE STUDY

Tom's Story: Tom came to me dealing with depression and overwhelming feelings for some considerable time. Despite efforts to get his life together, he felt like he was not making any progress. He continued to feel miserable. His hopelessness was exacerbated by having to finish a professional qualification. Overwhelmed by his lack of progress, he sunk deeper into depression. All of this impacted on his relationships and he struggled to maintain friendships. His focus on all aspects of his life was impeded. Even when he tried to work on his problems, they just seemed to raise further issues. He was now feeling completely stuck and isolated. He also felt his age was against him as a mature student. He compared his situation to the sinking of the Titanic: he was drowning and didn't know how to get himself out of the water.

What we did: Through Talking Therapy, Tom was able to separate out his problems and identify which ones needed attention first. Following on from Talking Therapy, we used the STAR Technique (see next page) to slow down his racing thoughts. This technique also enabled him to zoom out of the overwhelming picture he saw so he could take smaller steps that put him in the driving seat. After that, Tom engaged in Cognitive Behaviour Therapy (CBT) to recognise how his mind chatter was destructive in his life and then reframe to make the positive changes that resulted in his desire to live a happier, healthier life.

Results: Tom was now equipped with techniques that enabled him to self-assess his issues and reframe them so he could experience a more positive outcome. He was able to regain confidence to complete his professional qualification and he found energy once more to go out and pick up his old friendships as well as make new ones. Tom was now in control of his life.

♦ TOOLS AND TECHNIQUES

How to stop feeling so overwhelmed using the STAR Technique

Next time you're feeling overwhelmed, here's a simple technique to use called the STAR Technique:

S – SURVEY:

Interrupt your emotional overwhelm with the command **Stop and Clap** so you can pause whatever you're doing.

T – TAKE A BREATH

Notice your breathing for a second. Breathe in slowly through the nose, expanding the belly, and exhale slowly through your mouth. Repeat four times.

A – ASK yourself, 'Why am I thinking this thought?'

Journal your thoughts, emotions and physical sensations. What ideas do you notice? What emotions do you feel? How does your body feel? Start to build a bank of your awareness. Awareness creates action to change.

R – REFOCUS your Perspective as you tend to blow things out of proportion. Mindfully consider how you'd like to respond. Name one thing you can focus on right now that you can control.

The STAR Technique will enable you to slow down your racing thoughts and help you focus in from the overwhelming bigger picture, to small steps that you can control.

Cognitive Behaviour Therapy (CBT)

Talking Therapy looks at changing the way you see yourself and other people in your world. Recognising your negative mind chatter, how it affects you and the way you behave because of it, is vital for change. Your feelings, thoughts and behaviours are all linked; using CBT tools enable you to change them from negative to the positive.

Choose something different to what you usually do. Make time for yourself each day that is fun, relaxing or enjoyable. Allow time for activities by creating a healthy balance – which gives you a sense of achievement and helps you to connect. When you are stressed, you will spend more time doing things, and have less enjoyment and closeness to others.

For instance, if your neighbour passes you in the street without acknowledging you, you will interpret it several ways. You think you have done something to annoy your neighbour. What has upset them? What did you say or do? They were okay with you before, so why do they not like you now? This may lead you to feel stressed and uneasy. Your negative mind chatter will think, 'You won't know what to say'. Perhaps the voices are telling you that you'll make a fool of yourself – Anxiety. But in turn, if you don't say 'Hi', then she will think you are deliberately being aloof leading to anger!

A more positive response might be that she just didn't see you. CBT aims to get you to a point where you can 'do this yourself'.

Mindfulness

Just being in the moment, not stressing about the future or hyper-focused on the past... just being in the moment/ day/place that you are in 100%. That also means stop multitasking. Your brain can actually perform better when it's not being pulled in a bunch of different directions.

One of my other favourite techniques is a daily brain dump. It's like a messier form of journaling where you just write down everything that's stressing you out or that you can't stop thinking about.

Write to-do lists, thoughts, memories, worries – whatever is making you feel unhappy.

Get it out of your head and onto some paper. The more you practice this, the easier it gets, and the calmer life feels.

Narrative Questioning is a powerful tool used along with the 1-10 Scale, to use as soon as you become aware, then use a tool or technique. After this, redo the 1-10 Scale.

A question to ask yourself: how INTENSE is your mind chatter in YOUR current problem?

How intense is the feeling rational or reasonable with your negative mind chatter?

What is the likelihood you will take action – be constructive?

♦   **FINAL THOUGHTS**

Feeling overwhelmed is a universal emotion when you feel that you have bitten off more than you can chew. The answer is to declutter what is going on around you, focus on one thing at a time and ensure you take time out for yourself to recharge your battery so you can tackle all the things that are important in your life, one small bite at a time. Using a variety of techniques, including the STAR Technique, CBT and Mindfulness, can put you back in control. Use these the moment you feel any overwhelm creeping back into your life.

Andrea's Learning Alerts

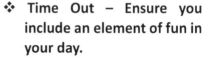

❖ Time Out – Ensure you include an element of fun in your day.

❖ Me Time – Ensure you take time out to do what you love.

❖ Overwhelm Cycle – Be aware of overwhelm cycle so you can break old patterns to create different results.

❖ STAR Technique – Use this any time you feel overwhelmed.

❖ CBT – Use this to change your perception.

❖ Journaling – A great way to dump feeling overwhelm.

❖ Mindfulness – Helps you focus on one thing with all your attention to change your thoughts and mood.

CHAPTER NINE
Guilt

'Guilt can either hold you back from growing, or it can show you what you need to shift in your life.'

Anon

Guilt is defined as 'the fact or state of having committed an offence, crime, violation, or wrong, especially against another person, moral or penal law'
(O.E.D)

D o you remember the first time you told a little white lie as a child? Somehow you found the courage to do something you had been told not to and realised that the ground did not open and swallow you. No doubt you will have been told many stories about what would happen if you told a lie: your nose will grow like Pinocchio's.

Guilt is a state that develops from outside influences within your culture, family and society into which you are born. Many people, including parents, use the 'guilt trip' as a form of control. As children, we naturally fall into the trap, and it is not until our cognitive development reaches the point where we understand right from wrong. In the UK, this is considered to be the age of 10.

Once you understand right from wrong, especially where other people are concerned, guilt is no longer an outside influence affected by the law, family and society. Still, as you develop your internal moral compass, you begin to feel guilt yourself rather than being told you should feel guilty. Here you start to live by values and principles, yet as people, we fail to acknowledge these in the beginning. It is often not until adulthood that you are forced by adverse circumstances to look inside and begin to explore who indeed you are.

♦ LET'S CONSIDER HOW GUILT IMPACTS YOUR BEHAVIOUR

When you feel guilty, emotion often leads to feeling stressed. This feeling occurs when you consistently let yourself or others down i.e. failing to meet your own or other people's expectations. You may feel a sense of crippling guilt if you miss a deadline. Guilt also occurs when you make an uncomplimentary comment to a friend or miss an opportunity to sign up a new client, or you are late for an important meeting. These are all things that niggle away at you.

Guilt shapes your perception, and you frequently believe you can work harder on tasks and activities. As an adult, outside influences still remain; no doubt you remember a time when the words 'You could have done better' echo in your mind. These words may have come from several trusted sources, such as your husband or partner, your family/kids, or your work. Guilt is sometimes self-imposed; your perception may not have lived up to your principles; you feel torn between needs of work and home, and not enough time to satisfy both areas of your life.

The Trickery of Guilt: HEALTHY v UNHEALTHY

You could consider healthy guilt as *correcting* something that plays with your moral compass. You know, when you offend your friend then realise, so you apologise. On the other hand, unhealthy guilt forms a *condemning perspective*. When things do not go your way often, your perception is that you see **you** as the problem, blame descends and you believe something is wrong with you. In this cycle, you enter a downward spiral towards more profound shame. Consequently, your stress levels elevate and anxiety follows. You irrationally go over and over the situation time and time again, even some years later if you do not address the situation when it first arises.

❖ **Healthy Guilt:** Some pangs of guilt allow you to step into the other person's shoes that you have offended and then experience empathetic feelings. These feelings are rational and proportionate to the situation or circumstance.

For example, some of your friends are going to have a party and have invited you. You intended to spend the evening with your best friend from school, but you decide to go to the party instead. You feel a pang of healthy guilt as you hurt your best friend's feelings, and you could have avoided hurting them. In these situations, you relate to your moral compass and as a result, usually apologise for your offending choices as the relationship is meaningful to you.

❖ **Unhealthy Guilt** forms from irrational and disproportionate feelings relative to a situation, often leaving you feeling you have no control. The same feelings emerge when you think your back is against the wall; you feel forced to make an unfavourable choice.

For example, you have just had a baby and are soon to return to work. While you long to stay at home with your baby, your financial circumstances do not allow you this luxury of being a stay-at-home mum. Your thoughts become irrational and disproportionate because you are not acting in line with your moral compass.

You also have the added social pressures of being a woman in today's modern society where being 'everything' is the expectation; everything to everyone, except you! The result is you live with incredible guilt. And if you are a parent, this guilt continues to appear every time you face a difficult situation regarding your child as it grows.

Brené Brown (American professor, lecturer and author): 'I'm just going to say it: I'm pro-guilt. Guilt is good. Guilt helps us stay on track because it's about our behaviour. It occurs when we compare something we've done — or failed to do — with our values. The discomfort that results often motivates real change, amends and self-reflection. ... If you made a mistake that hurt someone's feelings, would you be willing to say, "I'm sorry? I made a mistake."? If you're experiencing guilt, the answer is yes: "I *made* a mistake".'

Shonda Rhimes (Producer of Grey's Anatomy): 'Give yourself permission to fail. The guilt that we place on ourselves as parents are tremendous. I feel like we are supposed to be setting examples of strength, power, joy, and excitement for our children. And it's been really lovely to embrace that mindset both in how I'm parenting and in how I'm working.'

Julia Louis-Dreyfus (American Actress and Producer): 'The working-mom thing is tricky. Guilt is a bitch. It's so useless as an emotion, for me anyway. It clouds things, I'm not saying people shouldn't feel guilty, but for me, it makes specific decision-making more difficult. And I have felt guilty...'

'Most working mums are made to feel guilty when they have to return to work. I don't, as I love my job.'
Andrea Smith

♦ **THE POWER OF THE METAPHOR**

The Quicksand

This is a technique used by Steven C Hayes in his co-authored book, *Acceptance and Commitment Therapy* (ACT). When we're stuck in quicksand, the immediate impulse is to struggle and fight to get out. But that's precisely what you mustn't do in a swamp – because as you put the weight down on one part of your body (your foot), it goes deeper. So, the more you struggle, the deeper you sink – and the more you struggle. It is very much a no-win situation. With quicksand, there's only one option for survival. Spread the weight of your body over a large surface area – lay down. It goes against all our instincts to lie down and be with the quicksand, but that's precisely what we have to do. So it is with distress. We struggle and fight against it, but we've perhaps never considered just letting it be, and being with the distressing thoughts and feelings. Still, if we did, we'd find that we get through it and survive, more effectively than if we'd fought and struggled.

(Hayes et al. 1999)

Your instinct when struggling with guilt is to let it consume you like quicksand. Learning how to still yourself and dilute the feelings until they no longer affect you is vital to your mental health and well-being. Distancing yourself from the emotions is an excellent place to start, then you can accept them without judgement and, like an observer, allow them to pass.

A few years ago, due to my financial circumstances, I was working two jobs. Life was hectic in my home. My son and daughter were old enough to be at home alone. As I had no family in the UK, it became challenging to juggle home and family life. Part of the problem was I worked night shifts. As work was tough, the night shifts took its toll on me, making me feel overwhelmed; I was drained all of the time and felt exhausted as I had little sleep.

On top of working nights, I had to do the housework as well as shopping and cooking. I endured a feeling of enormous pressure. The most debilitating emotions were those associated with guilt. These feelings impacted my behaviour, and I became increasingly irritable, overwhelmed and stressed, including being overly strict with the children as my way of controlling the situation.

We as a family clashed on many occasions until I could no longer cope. Something had to give, and that's when I chose to give up the night shift work. It was time to take back control and create the life I wanted for my children and me.

♦ YOUR TURN

Go to your notebook/workbook. Identify a problem you overcame. Using Narrative Questions – What did you do? How did you feel? Why did things change for you? Journal it out without judgement. Come back after you have completed this activity.

♦ RELEASING GUILT

Guilt raises its head in many guises.

I should have followed the path I wanted for my life.

I'm an awful person for what I've done and the mistakes I've made.

I should have spent more time with my parents.

As we have previously discussed, guilt can be healthy or unhealthy. It's about learning how to let go and controlling the unhealthy guilt that can consume your life if you do not face it head-on. What others think and say is more likely to concern you than what you think about the situation yourself. You often find yourself looking over your shoulder at the neighbours. The illusion of life is warped by a skewed perception of both you and reality. All we truly ever see is a snapshot in time of what others are experiencing. The truth is that behind the smiles and closed doors, they too have feelings of guilt.

Guilt often is like being chained to a thought, a perception and a sense of responsibility. Consider ageing parents. Perhaps they also have ill health and are declining in their ability to remain in their own home. Having to make the massive decision to place your parent(s) in a nursing home is an all-consuming vehicle for guilt. Not only is that decision difficult, but you experience the domino effect of painful and challenging decisions around costs, quality, and even selling their home. In these circumstances, where the money is involved, it compounds the feelings of guilt. Sometimes you may choose to place your ageing parent in a less expensive home as you fear the dwindling impact on your inheritance.

No matter which decisions you make, guilt worms its way into your being. The alternative is to find ways of controlling the blame that allows you to accept it without feelings of guilt.

♦ IMPACT OF GUILT

A crushing sense of guilt can affect your physical health as well as your psyche. When you feel stressed, there is a release of the stress chemical cortisone, which will lead to headaches, aches and pains. But if you have been suffering from guilt for some time, it can impact your organs, including your heart, causing cardiovascular disease and even gastrointestinal disorders. Over time, this will actually damage your immune system.

Becoming aware of your emotions, thinking, physicality and behaviour with regards to guilty feelings, is the first step to creating change within. Knowing what guilt is and how it affects all of you is key to finding the courage to let it go and live guilt-free. The image below provides some of the impact guilt has on you – time to bring it to your attention so you can flip your thinking from negative to positive.

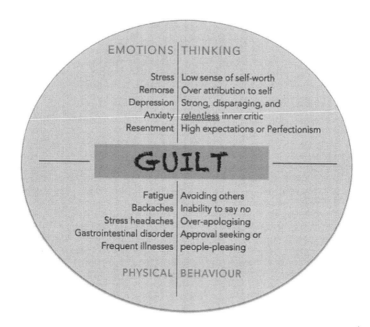

EMOTIONS	THINKING
Stress	Low sense of self-worth
Remorse	Over attribution to self
Depression	Strong, disparaging, and
Anxiety	relentless inner critic
Resentment	High expectations or Perfectionism

GUILT

Fatigue	Avoiding others
Backaches	Inability to say no
Stress headaches	Over-apologising
Gastrointestinal disorder	Approval seeking or
Frequent illnesses	people-pleasing
PHYSICAL	BEHAVIOUR

Emotions

With guilt comes a cocktail of emotions: stress, remorse, depression, anxiety and resentment. Without addressing these emotions and their cause, you continue to be in the downward spiral of guilt. *It's time to take action and change.*

Thinking

Your emotions inform your thinking, and you create a cacophony of imploding noise in your head; thoughts that do not make life enjoyable for you. Feelings such as a low sense of self-worth; over attribution to self; staunch disparaging, the relentless inner critic and high expectations, or being a perfectionist. *It's time to take action and change.*

Physical

Infused with negative emotions and thoughts, you soon begin to feel it rise within your body. Over time, fatigue, backaches, stress headaches, gastrointestinal disorder, and frequent illness invade your life. *It's time to take action and change.*

Behaviour

With everything negative going on in your mind, heart and body, it is no wonder that it soon impacts your behaviour. You begin to lose yourself and do not recognise the person you have become. You begin to avoid others; you find it difficult to say 'no'; you are continually apologising, whether it is your fault or not. All of these thoughts and actions result in you perpetually trying to please others and seeking approval for the smallest of tasks completed. *It's time to take action and change.*

CASE STUDY

Danny's Story: Danny's wife left him recently to live with someone else. He was devastated, but his most profound pain was that he missed his kids. He had a four-year-old girl and a six-year-old boy. He was very involved with the kids and spent time playing with them as much as he could. Danny helped them with their homework in the evening and read them a book every night when he put the children to bed. But his commitment with the kids meant that his wife felt left out and she moved in with an ex-boyfriend.

The separation left him financially unstable. Danny was a kind man and had an average paying job. His wife went back to living at the marital home with the kids so Danny had to find somewhere else to live. On top of that, he paid child maintenance to his ex-wife. Danny had responsibility for the lawyer's bill and all the excess fees. He was in financial and emotional trouble.

Consequently, Danny took on another job to deal with the financial mess. Regardless of this stress, all that mattered to him was the separation from his kids. He missed putting them to bed every night; doing their homework with them, and lost the little moments like waking up on a Sunday morning enjoying cuddles and mucking about.

He felt guilty as the kids did not understand what was happening: healthy guilt. The separation was also acrimonious, and there was much mud-slinging, saying some untruths about each other: unhealthy guilt. Danny was stressed and guilty in his inability to control his anger, irritability and unfairness of his situation. He did not know what to do.

What we did: Danny and I did Talking Therapy to discuss how his situation had changed and explored how he was dealing with it. Having introduced Narrative Questioning, he asked himself questions and journaled what thoughts and feelings arose for him. With the STRAIN technique (see next page), he was able to say 'no' to some unreasonable demands made by his ex-wife. As she was in a new relationship, some of the debt was now shared.

He started to look after himself and took control to remove his angry feelings. With new arrangements he made, Danny was now able to have alternative weekends with his kids. Danny was able to focus on this new routine for him and his kids, allowing him to re-engage with these significant relationships. With NLP and visualisation, Danny was able to empower himself with positive steps to start a new life.

Result: Danny now had a firm plan he was able to follow, enabling him to feel happier than he had in a long time. He was spending a lot of time with his kids, and he was grateful for the expert coaching advice he had received. Danny was also able to enter a friendly relationship with his ex-wife, which meant they were together doing positive things to co-parent their kids.

♦ TOOLS AND TECHNIQUES

When you feel guilty as an adult, chances are there have been bad feelings building since you were a child, so with these tools and techniques, it may take some time to unravel all the layers of the guilt.

Change your guilt and behaviour by starting with Small Steps: introducing the **STRAIN Technique**.

S *Say 'no'* – At first, you will feel uncomfortable doing this, but with any change comes discomfort. Saying 'no' allows you to put yourself first instead of last. When you first say 'no,' you will still have insecurities about it. Like everything else you want to get better at, with practice, you can build a bank of successes, so it becomes easier.

T *Take care of yourself* and take back control. Start by asking yourself: 'What are my expectations? What is good enough for me? How can I deal with all the responsibilities I have and still be okay with it?' Because remember, when you fall apart, you are not helpful to yourself or anyone else.

R *Re-evaluate* your expectations. For instance, you are rushing to attend an important meeting and are running late. Consider alternatives to this situation. Perhaps re-evaluate your time management and know that in future you have to begin getting ready earlier than usual. Strive to have everything you need prepared the night before and ensure you understand the route and exactly where you are going to avoid stress and guilt.

A *Assess* all situations for both achievement and failure. It is essential to acknowledge all of your accomplishments, no matter how small. Do not leave it to more noticeable results, such as securing a promotion. Celebrating all achievements is a great practice to build your self-esteem and self-worth.

I *Identify* where the 'guilt' voice comes from and ask yourself if it is Healthy Guilt or Unhealthy Guilt. Did you have a choice and did you do the best you could? Whether you had an opportunity or not, or you did the best you could, the answer is still the same; learn to accept it and let it go!

N *New learning.* Stop feeling guilty about making mistakes. View your failures or mistakes as a learning experience. When you assess what you perceive as a failure, this too is good practice because it allows you to learn from your mistakes. Once you are aware, you can then consider the alternative approaches to the situation rather than focus on the errors which may create feelings of stress and guilt. Remember, you are a 'good' person. Keep things in perspective.

Neurolinguistic Programming (NLP) is a therapeutic technique that can transform your self-limiting belief, empower you to take back control, and enable you to do something different, especially when it may feel uncomfortable. It allows you to move forward with a positive change. Breaking down your barriers and taking chances helps you to transform your life, leading to feeling happier and more satisfied with the things that you do.

NLP supports you to create a 'map' to illustrate how you see your situation, the people and events influencing your world. It is as if you wear goggles and you see only parts through those goggles: witnessing the same position with different perspectives. If two of you are standing side by side, looking at the same situation, you will both come out with a different experience. Whether you are aware of it or not, every situation and people that you meet along the way will impact your life in some manner. The impact will affect your beliefs, habits and actions as well as the choices you will make, including positively or negatively influencing your future.

Visualisation is a practical technique to influence your thoughts and feelings using your imagination to change your behaviours. You can use all your senses – smell, touch, hearing, sight and taste to visually create the movie that will inspire you to recreate a new way of acting, being and living.

The idea is to focus your mind on a pleasant and peaceful setting – use your mind and imagination. You are the movie maker and creator of your life so you can envision the potential of your situation and create new behaviours in your life. By using visualisation to see things differently, you can fashion a multisensory experience in your mind. The power of creative visualisation will open up new opportunities to create positive outcomes. You will picture positive results to help you create this reality in your life.

Narrative Questioning is a powerful tool used along with the 1-10 Scale. Use as soon as you become aware, then use a tool or technique to impact your challenge, after which redo the 1-10 Scale.

<u>**A question**</u> to ask yourself: how INTENSE is your feelings of guilt in YOUR current problem?

How intense is the impact rational or reasonable on your thinking and behaviour?

What is the likelihood you will take action – be honest?

♦   **FINAL THOUGHTS**

Guilt is a debilitating emotion developed by assuming family, cultural and community limiting beliefs around many topics. When you believe you cannot live up to other people's expectations, rules and moral codes, you begin to listen to your inner voice and experience feelings of guilt.

While guilt has a negative press, it can also support you in making better choices for yourself. In life, it is about developing your moral compass of what is right and wrong for you, as well as living harmoniously within a community. The STRAIN Technique, NLP techniques and visualisations are a few ways in which you can transform your guilt to a healthier perception of yourself.

Andrea's Learning Alerts

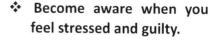

❖ Become aware when you feel stressed and guilty.

❖ Journal out your thoughts and feelings.

❖ Use NLP techniques to change your thinking patterns.

❖ See wins and failures as learning experiences.

❖ Use the STRAIN Technique.

❖ Visualise what you want.

❖ Practice reflection using the 1-10 Scale – take reading as soon as you are aware, use one of the tools and techniques, then redo the 1-10 Scale.

❖ Find a mentor, coach or therapist to work with you.

CHAPTER TEN
Creating Your Stress Resilience Map – Turning Fear into Freedom

'When we learn how to become resilient, we learn how to embrace the beautifully broad spectrum of human experience.'

Jaeda DeWalt
American Artist and Author of
'Chasing Desdemona'

You have no doubt heard various definitions for Stress Resilience. The American Psychological Association define it as 'the process of adapting well in the face of adversity, trauma, tragedy, threats or significant sources of stress – such as family and relationship problems, serious health problems or workplace and financial stressors.' It means 'bouncing back' from painful experiences. How can you bounce back in these circumstances? With love and guidance. That's why I created the Stress Resilience Map as a clear path to facing your fears, becoming stress-free and finding freedom.

Stress Resilience Map – A Complete and Comprehensive Programme Solution

When you get stuck in your emotional turmoil, it is time to seek help and take action. With guidance, finding a safe environment that allows you to dive deeper into your own well-being, you can begin to leave the old you behind and find the **real** you. That is why creating a Stress Resilience Map of the influential factors and/or people involved in your life, will enable you to revisit issues time and time again. With your Stress Resilience Map, you will learn how to uncover hidden solutions, bringing fresh perspectives.

Come with me on a transformational journey through the use of the Stress Resilience Map.

1. **Assessment and Identification of Challenges –** What's going on? It's a way in which you can gather information from different circumstances for you to develop a deep understanding of what is happening. Consider a work colleague who keeps telling you things about her troubled marriage and life. Over time, you feel stressed at work and it begins to wear you down. All the things she is telling you have been playing on your mind. It is disturbing your sleep, appetite and ability to focus.

2. **Psychological Evaluation –** Looking Glass is a self-assessment process in which you can look at yourself based on how you see yourself and how others see you.

3. **Environment Assessment –** Where am I? Are you emotionally reacting to something or someone about something painful, raw or unresolved? Identify and reflect the essential values you live your life by. Be honest. Observe how your friends and family interact with you. Let's say that arguing at home has become a regular occurrence. You and your husband live with your mother-in-law along with your two little children. You try hard to tidy up after your family, but it still affects your mother-in-law and her orderly habits. She resents you, and you are on guard as your mother-in-law's behaviour triggers a painful memory of how your mum used to overly judge you.

4. **Behavioural Response** – What do you do when you face feelings of stress? How you perceive and think about your trigger or stressor can make a significant impact.

5. **Triggers** – What are your 'pushing buttons'? Whether or not you experience an intolerable level of psychological stress depends on the intensity of the event or situation. Consider how you are at dealing with the stress. How you perceive and think about the stressor you are faced with can also make a significant impact on how you respond. It's not always possible to escape a stressful event or avoid a problem, but you can try to reduce the stress you are feeling. Evaluate whether you can change the situation that is causing you stress. Perhaps by dropping some responsibility, relaxing your standards or asking for help, it will create the change you seek.

6. **Mindset Training** – Training my thinking (decision-making). As your beliefs and assumptions change, so too will your mindset, thereby improving the reasoning used to solve the issues you face. Therefore, the actions you take will create better results. Sometimes your mindset can be shaped by changing one or more of the things that influence your beliefs, assumptions and decisions. When you fail at a specific time in your life, you may think it's because you lack healthy mental habits. By learning how to use thinking and reasoning to solve problems, you regain control. To develop healthy thinking, when your mindset is characterised by attributes such as work ethic, commitment, focus and honesty, you begin to develop a healthy mindset.

7. The Ease of Feeling Stress-free: Explore, Expose, Expand – My feelings: Being stress-free is about you taking control of your emotional thinking and resilience. There is a tendency towards denial, withdrawal and self-isolation, which are common reactions when you genuinely feel emotional pain. Consider the Ease of Feeling Stress-free.

Explore what is going on right in the moment of stress. Call out the emotions.

Expose them for what they signify and how they impact on your life. One clue that you are feeling distressed may be is when you become unusually quiet or shut down. Such silence speaks volumes, and generally the message is, 'I'm not going to risk you hurting me more than you already have... so I'm putting a wall between us.' On the contrary, it's also possible that you might suddenly become fidgety, restless, or hyper. You may attempt through activity to distract yourself from the hurtful words or behaviour (however inadvertently) caused by other people. You may unexpectedly lose your appetite or start eating voraciously to 'stuff' feelings or numb the pain. After all, you have at your disposal all sorts of defences to protect you from hurting.

Expand the opportunities and possibilities of the emotions exposed and shift perception to create the desired change.

By exploring, exposing and expanding all the feelings, you can identify your triggers and actions to adopt a resilient mindset for change.

8. **Reframe/Reprogramming Stress Responses –** Thinking differently. At the root of reframing and reprogramming, you begin to understand that your thoughts influence your intentions. You strive for acceptance of situations outside of your control. Thinking differently about each circumstance empowers you to develop a positive stress response.

9. **Decision-making –** Making positive choices. When you want to change your life, it is essential to understand that negative choices end up being counterproductive. These negative choices can quickly create a downward spiral into stress, overwhelm and guilt. On the other hand, making positive decisions leads to happier feelings, a sense of control and favourable outcomes The selection is natural when your 'why' is identified, when you have a goal to achieve, and a plan to keep you on the right path.

10. **Relationship Support –** Changed relationships. Strong social support can improve your resilience to stress. Friends or family can be good at listening and empathising. They may excel at practical help, like bringing over a home-cooked meal, or covering an hour of childcare. The question you have to ask yourself is, are they good at supporting you emotionally when you need it? Finding the 'right' support is essential. It can increase positive emotions which improve your decision-making, behaviour and sense of well-being. Without help, your life will be like Groundhog Day.

11. **Productivity –** Get more done. When you address your challenges with a positive mindset, your productivity

naturally increases, which leads you to feel more fulfilled and happier.

12. **Happy and Successful –** This is me! When you have taken the path of least resistance through using the Stress Resilience Map, you arrive at a new point in your life where you feel more like the real you. Gone is all the stress, and you craft a treasure chest of tips, skills and techniques that you can use any time you feel that life is getting on top of you once again.

Using a physical map will enable you to get to the core of your struggles. Additionally, becoming aware of your triggers allows you to confront them. You equip yourself with tools to manage your stress, overwhelm and guilt. You begin to relinquish judging yourself and others less, make better decisions, and communicate effectively. With improved communication, you express your emotions when you feel bad and manage your discomfort with greater success. Before you know it, your symptoms have lessened.

Feel empowered to get the results you intend. Awareness enables you to remove the deep layers of negativity and reveal who you indeed are. You are in control, and you can now externalise an inner image of the relationship problems, workplace challenges or crisis, or habit or behaviour patterns you wish to change. When you find a fresh, different perspective, it is easier to find a Step to Better.

◆ IMPACT OF USING THE STRESS RESILIENCE MAP

The four areas that will benefit from using the Stress Resilience Map are: *Physical*, *Mental*, *Emotional* and *Social Flexibility*.

Physical Flexibility: endurance, strength, having a clear sense of purpose, clear values, drive, and direction to help you to persist and achieve in the face of setbacks. The ability to withstand shock, protect your weak spots, and anticipate risk.

Mental Flexibility: the ability to focus, adapt to change, increase your attention span, incorporate multiple points of view. Problem solving, adapting, and being flexible to the evolving situations which are beyond your control are essential to maintaining resilience. Your ability to cope with change and recover is your new power.

Emotional Flexibility: a positive outlook, protect your weak spots, self-regulation, having feelings of competence, effectiveness in coping with stressful situations, and healthy self-esteem are inherent to feeling resilient. The frequencies with which you experience positive and negative emotions are fundamental.

Social Flexibility: Building a good relationship with others and a support system that can help you overcome adverse situations, rather than cope on your own.

The Stress Resilience Map allows you to identify the core of your struggles. It creates a non-judgemental space to explore and address the root causes. It paves a path of least resilience by providing a problem-solving tool kit.

Learning Ignites Creativity: Apart from what I studied at university, I worked hard for the last 10 years to learn. I learnt through personal therapy, attending courses and meeting up with like-minded people, engaging in group therapy and learning from my peers. Life taught me many lessons through failing at many things, falling down, and dealing with the fear, pain and loneliness. Like many other people, I experienced anxiety about money. Questions filled my mind, such as 'How will I manage the mortgage? What will happen if I get injured or cannot work?'

I found that I was resilient from the inside; I had patience and courage to bring up two kids with no family, close friends or support. I found my own power that came from inside me. And the perception came to me that I was stronger than I felt on many occasions.

As my journey toward discovering how to deal with life's challenges relating to stress, overwhelm and guilt continues, I will walk you further into my life. There have been numerous ups and downs; talking about it here has not been easy, but I wanted you to know that I have been where you are right now.

♦ YOUR TURN

Go to your notebook/workbook. Identify a problem you overcame. Using Narrative Questions – What did you do? How did you feel? Why did things change for you? Journal it out without judgement. Come back after you have completed this activity.

♦ **LOVE, LIGHT AND LAUGHTER**

'You start living the moment you decide your life is yours – and not anyone else's.'
Adel Forsythe
Founder, WholeheartedWomen.org

What is the Meaning of Life? Why are we here? These are the deepest questions most humans ask themselves at some point in their life. Our views shaped by our beliefs, culture, religion, science and experiences, determine what we consider as 'truth'. When you ask people from around the world how they want to feel in life, they often answer 'happy, healthy and free'.

Most people understand that life is a journey. Some describe it as being on a path, others see it as a road that unfolds, and perhaps you have your idea of your journey through life. Whatever you think about life, it certainly is paved with ups and downs. The undulating journey of life is filled with lessons, hardships, heartaches, joys, celebrations and special moments. The roller coaster of life can be both exhilarating and debilitating, depending upon your experiences, levels of resilience and mental capacity to cope with ever-changing landscapes.

One of the vital secrets to avoiding stress in your life is to take the focus away from the negative thoughts, feelings and behaviour. Learn how to switch it to centre on what makes you feel happy and fulfilled. If you want your adult mind reprogrammed, then I suggest you revisit your inner child who loved to laugh, play and explore life with excited curiosity. It is indeed a universal consensus that laughter feeds the soul. With that in mind, let us further explore how you can infuse more Love, Light and Laughter into your life today.

♦ **LOVE**

'Falling in love with myself. All flaws included.'
Dau Voire
Blogger and social media influencer

What is 'love'? Love is a force of nature. It is unpredictable, and you cannot control who you love or who loves you. But what you can do is learn to love yourself more. Loving yourself is vital to your absolute happiness. When you first fill up your love cup, then you can begin to let the overflow reach others, even those you find it difficult to like.

Love does terrific things for your state of mind, and it is also a natural stress reliever.

Remember those first flutterings of love when you met your partner? Or the love that exudes when you look at a newborn baby? For many people, they feel a deep love for their animals too. When you are in these states of high emotion, your brain releases oxytocin, or the feel-good factor hormone. Our 'happy hormones' also include the release of dopamine, which increases your levels of serotonin, leaving you with a surge of positive emotion.

Our goal is to be able to turn on our happy hormones before we are sucked into the negative emotions associated with stress, overwhelm and guilt. You are in the driving seat of your life, and it is your responsibility to ensure that you have a suitable tool kit to help you maintain loving feelings.

Doing what you love in life is essential for your mental health and well-being. Connect to that childlike sense of awe and wonder which you find in the simple things of life, such as sunrises and sunsets, nature and creativity. The secret key is to love what you do and do what you love – even the little things like eating delicious food, sharing moments with special people and reading a book.

◆   **LIGHT**

'Happiness can be found even in the darkest of nights, if one only remembers to turn on the light.'
Harry Potter and the Prisoner of Azkaban
J.K. Rowling

What comes to your mind when you hear the word 'light'? Do you consider it a means to illuminate the darkness? Do you connect it with the weight of something like a feather? Or do you think of it as a vibrancy that radiates from the rainbow sparkle of a diamond?

Often when people hear the word 'light', they think of the religious connotations of Christ in Christianity. Light symbolises many things, such as hope, intelligence and goodness. These concepts are very much part of keeping stress at bay. When you experience the light of long summer nights, you feel more uplifted and safer. You have more energy and feel motivated to engage in more physical activities. All of these things benefit your ability to remain stress-free and in a state of well-being.

One of the most fundamental sources of light is the sun. It is essential, therefore, that you experience as much sunlight for your mental and physical health. The sun provides you with vitamin D which is vital for calcium absorption, nerve conduction and immune function; it is one of the body's most essential nutrients. When you nourish yourself with good sunlight, it affects your feel-good factor which protects you against stress. Being in nature is vital to sustaining you inside and out, for both your physical and mental well-being.

Light is also an energy force. Without light from the sun, you would have no food to nourish your body and soul. Remember the love and pleasure you can receive from enjoying a delicious meal with friends and loved ones? Light is also needed for us to see. Stress, overwhelm, and guilt is like living in a darkened world. Hence, accepting the need for light in your life is essential for you to take control of seeing what is vital to enable you to live stress-free. For me, light allows us to see the magical colours of this wonderful world. Looking at the colours of nature ignites the awe and wonder of that inner child once more where stress cannot reside. Find shade in your life to lighten your mood and keep you in high spirits.

♦ LAUGHTER

'Laughter is and will always be the best form of therapy.'
Dau Voire
Blogger and social media influencer

One of the best strategies for stress management is laughter. The best part is that is it's free! Numerous studies highlight how laughter boosts your health and seems to melt all your troubles away.

Do you know when you laugh, it lowers your stress hormone levels? It decreases the epinephrine (adrenaline) and cortisol in the bloodstream, by increasing the levels of health-boosting hormones, such as endorphins, dopamine and oxytocin. Can you remember a time when you laughed heartily and would be able to recall it throughout your day? This lingering sense illustrates the ripple effect of the feel-good factor that laughing induces.

When you bask in the well-being of laughter, it strengthens your immune system and can even relieve pain. Laughter has an enhancing ability to keep other diseases at bay. Your antibody-producing cells increase, and you are protected from the physical effects of stress.

When you are faced with a situation that you find threatening, it raises stress levels. Finding something to laugh about can help you take a more light-hearted approach.

Consider some of the following strategies that you can use when faced with a challenge.

1. **Make including fun into your day a non-negotiable choice.**

   Committing 100% to this choice will improve your self-esteem too. The physical impact of laughter is like having a great physical workout without going to the gym. It improves your heart and lungs, and leaves your muscles more relaxed. The list is endless. Tell jokes. Watch comedies. Read joke books.

2. **Always look on the bright side of life!**

   As Monty Python said! They knew a thing or two about having a good sense of humour as it encourages more laughter in your life. With a cheerful outlook, you will decrease your levels of stress. You could even join a laughter yoga club near you.

3. **Watch your favourite comedy show or movie.**

   Technology today allows you to access films and TV shows when you choose. With so much streaming on TV, phones and tablets, you can explore new shows that you find hilarious. Look for shows that are not just marginally funny, but entertaining.

4. **Laughing with friends elevates your mood.**

   Laughing together improves not only your mood but the quality of your relationships and interactions. Go with friends to a comedy club as an entertaining way to get more laughter in your life. When you laugh, you find it has a heightened contagious effect; when you hear a belly laugh, you cannot resist joining in.

5. Find humour in all things, even those you would typically complain about.

Look for the humour in life events and situations, whether good or bad. Being able to see the fun releases you from the pain that stress produces. Laughing about sombre things does not minimise the seriousness of a matter; it allows you to detach and change your perspective, leading to a positive attitude. You can still find happiness, even when you are facing challenges. Develop a good sense of humour; it's a gift.

6. Laugh or smile without reason.

You've heard the phrase 'Fake it until you make it' – it works! Your subconscious mind cannot distinguish between real and fake, so you may as well pretend to feel happy rather than being miserable. Also, you cannot feel negative emotions when you smile. Try it! You and your body and brain are wired for happiness. Your body already knows this; now let this truth sink into your mind. Smile, and enjoy life.

7. Remember to make your fun and laughter healthy!

While laughing and having fun is a marvellous way to feel good, remember not to laugh at the expense of someone else's feelings. Healthy fun has excellent benefits but reminds you to protect your mind. With good pleasure, there is no aftermath of negative consequences to deal with, such as a hangover, added debt, a hurt loved one, or damage to key relationships.

When you fill your life with Love, Light and Laughter, you shift your perspective and feel less troubled. Your perception also changes, resulting in being a great person to be around. Making a conscious choice to live this way elevates the happy hormones, and ultimately you will enjoy and benefit more from your life.

Consider the benefits of including more Love, Light and Laughter

❖ Reducing the level of stress hormones like cortisol and increases endorphins together with antibody-producing cells means we have a more robust immune system.

❖ The physical and emotional release will occur when you laugh, love and feel good. You will experience a cleansed feeling after a good laugh.

❖ Love, light and laughter will exercise your diaphragm and works out the chest muscles, leaving you feeling relaxed, and it's also great for your heart.

❖ Good feelings can bring a distraction: your focus is away from stress, overwhelm, guilt, anger and negative mind chatter.

❖ Your response to stressful events can be altered by whether you can view the threat felt in the stress response. Laughter can put into perspective your stress, and love and light can help you see situations or events as challenges and less threatening.

❖ Many social benefits help when you feel good; laughter makes other people smile and fills you with love and light. Elevating the mood with the joy you feel around those around you will reduce their stress levels as well, and improve social interaction. Laughter is glue that draws like-minded into the fold, where happiness will spread through you. Laughter is not primarily about humour, but it's about social relationships. Laughter have been shown to diminish stress and connect us to others, making life more fun. When you laugh together, it puts you at ease with each another.

❖ When positive emotions are increased, it makes it easier for you to go on to wholeness and disease-free living.

**'Live conscious of every moment,
and the wonder available in it.'**
TemitOpe Ibrahim
Author of 'The Secrets to Your Win'

♦ **CONSCIOUS LIVING – BECOMING AWARE OF YOUR WORLD**

When you hear the term 'living consciously', does it bring up healthy foods, environmental activist, psychics, mystics? That is a misconception. Most of you can practice living consciously – living from the inside out. It can benefit the environment, improve your health physically, emotionally and mentally, your relationships and your social environment. When you become aware of how to live consciously, you can begin to practice it daily. This conscious choice does not mean you have to massively change your lifestyle. Instead, just to pay attention to the world around you.

The importance of becoming aware of your world is a habit you need to develop if you want to live stress-free. Make time each day to switch off from the busyness of life through Mindful Being and make it part of your daily routine. Life's daily routines include such activities as going to work, cooking, cleaning and looking after your family. You do these activities on autopilot, day and night. When you become more aware of each place, action and thing, you learn to appreciate each one for its beauty, simplicity and wonderment. Consider some of these everyday occurrences that you can apply Mindfulness to:

❖ When you adopt the discipline of living consciously, it will lead you to make better choices. You become more mindful about the food with which you fuel your body, recycling materials to improve the planet, and walking more rather than jumping in the car.

❖ Becoming aware of how you spend your time will make a difference in achieving your goals and productivity. You will make positive choices that will benefit you, others and the planet. You take more responsibility for your decisions and outcomes through increased diligence to the areas that help your personal development and are essential to you.

❖ Be grateful for everything you have in your life, good and bad, and appreciate the lessons that it teaches you. Enjoy the world around you and begin to notice all the nuances in nature, yourself and relationships.

◆ ADOPTING A NEW APPROACH: MINDFULNESS

In today's fast changing pace of life, work plays an important role and with that comes pressure in the form of stress, overwhelm and guilt. Mindfulness can significantly improve your habits and negative mind chatter. Therefore, with Mindfulness your social life, mind and body relaxation and calmness can benefit too. Just like plants need water, nutrients and sunlight, your mind needs to be nurtured too. Mindfulness will create a calm mind; clear away distractions, and reduce stress-inducing emotions. You learn to sharpen your focus leading you to live life on your terms.

Mindfulness is defined as 'the basic human ability to be fully present, aware of where we are and what we are doing, and not overly reactive, stressed or overwhelmed by what's going on around us.' (mindful.org)

Mindfulness as a practice is not as easy as the picture painted in the media and magazines. However, if it is practiced daily, Mindfulness will bring awareness via your senses, to your thoughts, feelings, and behaviours or actions.

The goal of Mindfulness is to wake up your senses of your physical, mental and emotional processes. Your mind is very good at creating thoughts and feelings or emotions that are stuck and demand your attention. Judgemental attitudes come to you and are out your control.

It's so easy to see experiences or people through the prism of the labels you carry over from the past. Conscious Living using a mindful approach will bring a fresh and new perspective, including many benefits. It can help you reduce stress and improve your health and well-being.

♦ HOW CONSCIOUS LIVING AFFECTS YOUR LIFE, OTHERS AND THE WORLD

Many people are motivated by money, culture, traditions and family, and live unconsciously by their rules. When you awaken your awareness to your world, you begin to see beyond the materialism, consumerism and limiting beliefs as part of your upbringing. However, to unlock your potential, Mindfulness and living consciously are necessary. It is essential to ask questions and ponder on how you live your life. Do you feel content and happy? Do you feel healthy? Do you spend enough time with loved ones and family?

If the answer to some of your questions is 'no', then you can identify the areas to improve through increased awareness. Whether it's some quiet time to practice Mindfulness, meditation or journaling, think and reflect deeply about the things that matter to you and are close to your heart. Ask yourself where you can be more conscious. Reflect on how you have spent your day, and where your time could be better spent tomorrow. If you have become aware that you need to exercise more or eat better, change the things you can. Maybe you have decided to follow a passion or set a new goal; make daily reminders to take small steps towards it.

Mindfulness is about forming fresh perspectives by exploring new sources of information. Becoming aware, reflect, read, and watch enlightening and inspirational videos so you can learn and grow. Mindfulness empowers you to think about yourself and the world differently.

For you to change your lifestyle to one focused on Conscious Living can take time and determination. Changing your life is a process that is more than worth the effort. With a greater understanding of yourself and your inner thoughts and feelings, you can take actions that benefit you and those around you. Conscious Living allows you the opportunity to connect with yourself, your environment, and the people you care about, and it gives you real power over your life.

I would encourage you to find someone you can look up to during your journey. Tony Robbins has inspired me during times of challenge. In his words, in *Awaken the Giant Within*, 'Using the power of decision gives you the capacity to get past any excuse to change any and every part of your life in an instant.'

With these lasting words echoing in your mind, I inspire you to Fear Less, Live More!

Think!

If you think you are beaten, you are,

If you think you dare not, you don't,

If you like to win, but you think you can't,

It's almost certain you won't

If you think you'll lose, you're lost,

For out of the world we find,

Success begins with a person's will

It's all a state of mind

If you think you are outclassed you are,

You've got to think high to rise,

You've got to be sure of yourself before

You can ever win a prize

Life's battles don't always go

To the strongest or fastest person

But sooner or later the person who wins

Is the one who thought they could

Walter D Windle, American Poet

Afterword

Thank you for taking the time to buy and read *Fear Less, Live More*.

The vision I created for this book and you was to build a community, and to empower you to be able to transform your Stress, Overwhelm and Guilt into extraordinary success, happiness and freedom.

I included many of the tools, techniques and strategies developed over 20 years of expertise, experience and learning that I use today when working with my clients, as demonstrated in the Case Studies. This intentional inclusion would allow insight into what it takes to change your mindset, perception and behaviour in your life.

In order to create deep and meaningful change in your life requires the skill and expertise of a certified therapist and coach. When you work with a certified therapist, you can be assured that you are in safe hands. They are able to take you safely to vulnerable, dark places in your life and gently guide you to a new way of thinking, feeling and acting. As a coach, I can then build on this healing and work with you to show you how you can achieve what you once thought was impossible.

I have developed my signature programme 'The Ultimate Stress Resilience Programme' so you can benefit from the practical strategies contained within this book. To find out more about this, and other ways in which I can support and work with you, visit my website www.andreaasmith.com for further details.

You can join my free Facebook Group 'Making Life Better' (www.facebook.com/group/makinglifebetter) where you can meet like-minded individuals with similar experiences. You will have my support and guidance and access to free resources. The outcome of my work is to create more Stress Resilient individuals who can live life on their terms and are ready with a toolbox of strategies when life throws up challenges.

It is my intention that you will have more access to my products and services so you can Fear Less, Live More.

Andrea A Smith

Connect with me:
https://andreaasmith.com/
hello@andreaasmith.com
www.facebook.com/group/makinglifebetter

References

CHAPTER 1

Betsy Hayes – brain image based on Illustration by Betsy Hayes

Nick Owen, Dances with Wolves - More Magic of Metaphors – Crown House Publishing, 2004

Your Persistent Positive Focus – Have a Magnificent Day! https://www.beliefnet.com/columnists/haveamagnificentday/2014/01/your-persistent-positive-focus.html

CHAPTER 2

Difference between Anxiety and Stress | Anxiety vs Stress. http://www.differencebetween.info/difference-between-anxiety-and-stress

19 Narrative Therapy Techniques, Interventions .... https://positivepsychology.com/narrative-therapy/

https://www.healthline.com/health/anxiety-exercises

https://www.counselling-directory.org.uk/memberarticles/the-anxiety-experience-7-metaphors-to-illustrate-anxiety

https://www.safespaceconnect.com/panic-disorder

Panic disorder, NHS. https://www.nhs.uk/conditions/panic-disorder/

Panic attacks | Mind, the mental health charity - help for .... https://www.mind.org.uk/information-support/types-of-mental-health-problems/anxiety-and-panic-attacks/panic-attacks/

Fight, Flight, or Freeze: How We Respond to Threats. https://www.healthline.com/health/mental-health/fight-flight-freeze

How Hormones Affect Panic Attacks and Anxiety? Four Stress .... https://www.bigmindstory.com/how-hormones-affect-panic-attacks-and-anxiety/

Fight Flight Freeze: How To Recognize It And What To Do https://www.betterhelp.com/advice/trauma/fight-flight-freeze-how-to-recognize-it-and-what-to-do-when-it-happens/

https://www.betterhelp.com/advice/trauma/fight-flight-freeze-how-to-recognize-it-and-what-to-do-when-it-happens/

CHAPTER 3

https://www.verywellmind.com/the-purpose-of-emotions-2795181

https://www.thefreedictionary.com/Beliefs

https://pediaa.com/difference-between-mental-and-emotional/

words – The Holistic Journal. https://theholisticdirectory.wordpress.com/tag/words/

Difference Between Mental and Emotional | Meaning .... https://pediaa.com/difference-between-mental-and-emotional/

How To Break The Cycle Of Negative Emotions - Unlimited Choice. https://unlimitedchoice.org/coaching/negative-emotions/

Why Stress Makes It Harder to Control Emotions | Live Science. https://www.livescience.com/39177-stress-emotion-control.html

CHAPTER 4

What is the Law of Attraction? A Complete Guide | Tony Robbins. https://www.tonyrobbins.com/business/law-of-attraction/

80 % of Thoughts Are Negative…95 % are repetitive – The https://faithhopeandpsychology.wordpress.com/2012/03/02/80-of-thoughts-are-negative-95-are-repetitive/

Quote by Sun Tzu: 'If you know the enemy and know yourself ….' https://www.goodreads.com/quotes/17976-if-you-know-the-enemy-and-know-yourself-you-need

Challenging Assumptions Reframing Metaphor – Best Hypnosis …. https://besthypnosisscripts.com/metaphor-therapy/reframing-metaphors/challenging-assumptions/

Hayes et al 1999), Metaphors for Therapy - Getselfhelp. co.uk. https://www.getselfhelp.co.uk/metaphors.htm

CHAPTER 5

The Right Question Reframe Metaphor – Best Hypnosis Scripts. https://besthypnosisscripts.com/metaphor-therapy/reframing-metaphors/right-question/

How to Cope With Emotions Using Distraction. https://www.verywellmind.com/coping-with-emotions-with-distraction-2797606

CHAPTER 6

Kiirkas – The Planning, Development, and Implementation of .... http://kiirkas.com/

Suicidal Thoughts and Behaviours in People With BPD. https://www.verywellmind.com/suicidality-in-borderline-personality-disorder-425485

How to Manage When We Feel Overwhelmed | Talkspace. https://www.talkspace.com/blog/feeling-overwhelmed/

How to Name, Shame and Then Let It Go. https://www.counseling.org/news/aca-blogs/aca-member-blogs/aca-member-blogs/2019/05/23/how-to-name-shame-and-then-let-it-go

Therapy for Guilt - GoodTherapy.org. https://www.goodtherapy.org/learn-about-therapy/issues/guilt

The Anxiety Experience: 7 metaphors to illustrate anxiety https://www.counselling-directory.org.uk/memberarticles/the-anxiety-experience-7-metaphors-to-illustrate-anxiety

How to Manage When We Feel Overwhelmed | Talkspace. https://www.talkspace.com/blog/feeling-overwhelmed/

The anxiety experience: 7 metaphors to illustrate anxiety https://www.counselling-directory.org.uk/memberarticles/the-anxiety-experience-7-metaphors-to-illustrate-anxiety

How to Manage When We Feel Overwhelmed | Talkspace. https://www.talkspace.com/blog/feeling-overwhelmed/

CHAPTER 7

Is Stress Affecting You in The Workplace? | SMALL BUSINESS CEO. http://www.smbceo.com/2017/05/08/workplace-stress/

List Of Good Common Therapeutic Metaphors – Examples For https://www.wellnessonfire.com/2017/10/08/list-of-good-common-therapeutic-metaphors-examples-for-healing/

What Causes IT Burnout? | BairesDev. https://www.bairesdev.com/blog/it-burnout/

The Warning Signs of Burnout - Overwhelming Stress .... https://app.assistertselvhjelp.no/en/warning-signs-of-burnout

CHAPTER 8

Mental health at work: The cost of 'boys being boys' — The https://thebigstorypodcast.ca/2019/03/06/wsib/

https://www.getselfhelp.co.uk/metaphors.htm

Art by Anna Brones https://annabrones.com/tag/art/page/2/

Five Ways to Stop a Worry-Filled What-If Cycle. https://psychcentral.com/blog/5-ways-to-stop-a-worry-filled-what-if-cycle/ (www.psychcentral.com)

How to stop feeling overwhelmed and hopeless : SuicideWatch. https://www.reddit.com/r/SuicideWatch/comments/8md8wt/how_to_stop_feeling_overwhelmed_and_hopeless/

Blog - Agony Assistant. https://www.agonyassistant.com/blog/

Cognitive Behaviour Therapy - Getselfhelp. https://www.get.gg/cbt.htm

CHAPTER 9

Mental health at work: The cost of 'boys being boys' — The https://thebigstorypodcast.ca/2019/03/06/wsib/

Quotes From 25 Famous Women on Guilt - The Cut. https://www.thecut.com/2017/09/quotes-from-25-famous-women-on-guilt.html

Guilt Quotes To Help You Overcome And Move On | Betterhelp. https://www.betterhelp.com/advice/guilt/guilt-quotes-to-help-you-overcome-and-move-on/

Therapy Metaphors - Getselfhelp.co.uk. https://www.getselfhelp.co.uk/docs/Metaphors.pdf

CHAPTER 10

What is Resilience – Building Resilience. https://building-resilience.com/what-is-resilience/

Cannon, Hosea. 'Be in Good Health.' American Jails, vol. 33, no. 2, American Jail Association, May 2019, p. 78.

Krasl Art Center welcomes a new exhibition.... https://www.wmta.org/2019/09/11/krasl-art-center-welcomes-a-new-exhibition-devoted-to-the-process-of-adapting-well-in-the-face-of-adversity-trauma-tragedy-threats-and-stress/

Healthy ways to handle life's stressors. https://www.apa.org/topics/stress-tips

More than Mindset: The Backbone is Here | HuffPost. https://www.huffpost.com/entry/more-than-mindset-the-backbone-is-here_b_5780157fe4b05b4c02fc80fc

BPD Distress Tolerance Skills - Verywell Mind. https://www.verywellmind.com/distress-tolerance-skills-for-bpd-425372

'Spirit of the Age.' The Week, no. 999, Dennis Publishing Ltd., Nov. 2014, p. 8.

7 Ways To Use Laughter to Lower Stress. https://blogs.
psychcentral.com/relationships/2018/11/7-ways-to-use-
laughter-to-lower-stress/

Your Best Health Care: Health Care and Laughter. https://
yourbesthealthcare.blogspot.com/2009/04/health-care-
and-laughter.html

Laugh Often and Unleash the Benefits | Ornish Lifestyle
https://www.ornish.com/zine/the-health-benefits-of-
laughter/

Mindfulness Class – Hospice & Community Care. https://
hospicecommunitycare.org/event/mindfulness-class-
2/?instance_id=1715

About Mindfulness — Mindfulness is a Superpower.
https://www.mindfulnessisasuperpower.com/team

Tony Robbins - Using the power of decision gives you
the.... https://www.brainyquote.com/quotes/tony_
robbins_173241

Quote by Walter D. Wintle: 'If you think you are beaten
....' https://www.goodreads.com/quotes/1033193-if-you-
think-you-are-beaten-you-are-if-you

Further Reading

Walter Bradford Cannon, *The Wisdom of the Body*, Revised edition, W.W. Norton, 1963.

Steven C Hayes, Kirk Strosahl, Kelly Wilson, *Acceptance and Commitment Therapy*, 2nd edition, Guilford Press, 2016.

Daniel Kahneman and Amos Tversky, 'The framing of decisions and the psychology of choice', *Science*, 30 Jan 1981: Vol. 211, Issue 4481, pp. 453-458.

Tony Robbins, *Awaken the Giant Within*, New edition, Simon & Schuster, 2001.

Kamal Sarma, *Mental Resilience: The Power of Clarity*, 2nd revised edition New World Library, 2008.

About the Author

Andrea Smith is a highly sought-after Certified Coach, Author and Speaker. With a 20 plus year Psychological and Medical well-being background, she is experienced to assess and coach people with many challenges around stress and anxiety disorders.

Shift your mindset

Andrea's purpose and passion are to help people to shift their mindset, so they can build *emotional resilience* when faced with everyday stresses and challenges. Having worked with numerous clients using her unique *Stress Resilience Coaching Techniques*, Andrea's Professionalism, Honesty, and Expertise ensure that change happens by going deeper into their well-being.

My Journey – No Plain Sailing

Andrea's personal challenges, including divorce, moving countries and being a single mum, provided her with the *strength* to build her resilience, allowing her to *bounce back* from *adversity*, becoming happy and *successful* in life

Extensive Qualification

Andrea's extensive training, experiences and unique medical background allows her to help you turn your fear into freedom, living your life on your terms. Andrea has a Masters in Psychology (BPS), a Registered Nursing Degree (NMC) with a 20-year acute hospital experience, Degree in Clinical Hypnosis, Master Neurolinguistic Programming (NLP) and is a Certified Life Coach and Speaker.

Impassioned, Andrea is building a community of empowered individuals, transforming Stressed, Overwhelmed and Guilty women in life and business. She enables them to experience extraordinary success, happiness and freedom – *Making Life Better*.